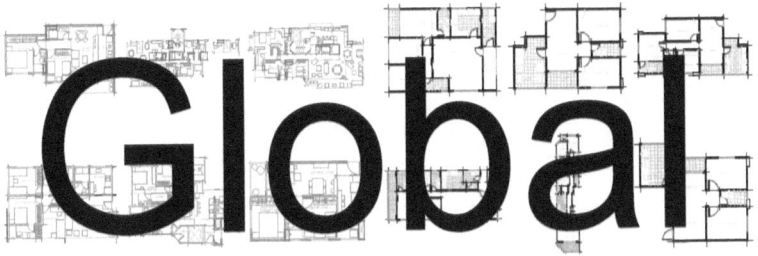

Global

Apartments

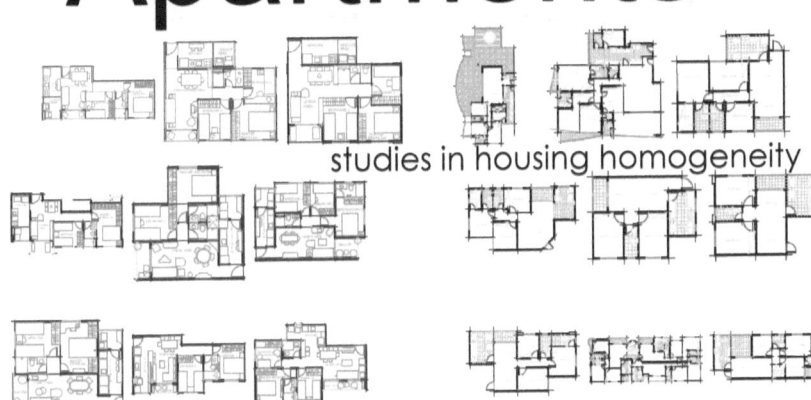

studies in housing homogeneity

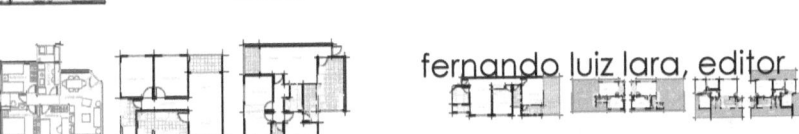

fernando luiz lara, editor

2009

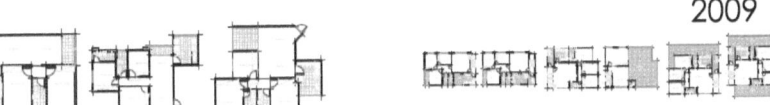

Global Apartments
studies in housing homogeneity

 Studio Toró

2009

published by Fernando Luiz Lara, Studio Toró and the Global Apartments Research Group at the University of Michigan's Taubman College of Architecture using Lulu.com, fonts Helvetica, Garamond and Antique Olive Roman, texts by the authors, reproduced here with permission. Translations by Fernando Luiz Lara, Alida Perrine and Elizabeth Martins.

ISBN 978-0-578-02454-7

1. Architecture. 2. Apartments. 3. Modern Movement.

English / Portuguese

www.studiotoro.org

Acknowledgements

This book is the result of almost a decade of research on multi-family buildings, known worldwide as apartments[1] After finishing my doctoral dissertation[2] on the unique appropriation of modernism in Brazil I got back to my native country and started teaching in Belo Horizonte. It was there, at the Catholic University's Graduate Program in Spatial Information Treatment that this research germinated. The original idea was to bring spatial analysis tools to the understanding of housing typologies or what Prof. João Francisco Abreu labeled "household geography" or *geografia do domicilio* in Portuguese. Using census data and GIS software to study housing arrangements would bridge together my architectural training and my phd work on modernism dissemination, taking the investigation to a broader scale in order to allow the research to be generalized and the data to be more reliable than the average architectural research.

It was at PUC-Minas between 2001 and 2002 that I started gathering data and collecting apartment plans. A initial grant from the PUC research funds (FIP 2002) turned into a larger grant from the Brazilian Council for Research (CNPq) awarded in 2003 when I was teaching at the Federal University of Minas Gerais. This initial data collection gave me the confidence to continue and tested my initial analysis, basically demonstrating that those first 200 apartments were similar to the point of having almost exactly the same graph spatial organization.

---

[1] In the US the word apartments usually mean rental units while the word condo is used for owner-occupied units. In most of the world which is the focus of our research the term apartments does not imply ownership or lease, meaning just a unit inside a multi-family building.
[2] The dissertation defended in 2001 became the basis of a book: LARA, Fernando, The Rise of Popular Modernist Architecture in Brazil, Gainesville: University of Florida Press, 2008.

In 2004, when I came to the University of Michigan, I thought of continuing this line of research but didn't have a very clear idea of how to keep researching Brazilian housing from 8000 kilometers away. The interaction with students of so many different nationalities indicated very early on that what I was talking about was not just a Brazilian trend but a global one. The interest with which students from South Korea, India, Russia and Egypt embraced the discussion of those ideas encouraged me to take this research to a global level.

The Global Apartments Research Group was born from this convergence of interests. I was very curious to learn about apartments in different parts of the planet and many international students were excited that, at last, a professor was interested in the contemporary built environment of their native lands. For 4 years (2005-2009) we met regularly (twice a month for most of the academic year) and discussed multi-family housing solutions in 13 different countries (Brazil, Costa-Rica, India, Mexico, Egypt, Finland, Italy, South Korea, Russia, Germany, US, Turkey, Japan). Short seminars taught in Belo Horizonte (2006) and Natal (2007) in Brazil and in Seoul, Korea (2007) gave me the chance to refine our hypothesis with a juicier local immersion.

Together we learned that the apartments are indeed very similar, despite being built in opposing parts of the world and housing families as diverse as Brazilians, Egyptians or Koreans. In 2006 a grant from Michigan's Office for the Vice President for Research (OVPR) allowed me to organize the data collection in a more productive way and support student summer work on analyzing parts of the data, some of which became chapters in this book. I also had the opportunity to teach a seminar on Housing Design twice during this time that helped stir student interest and solidify the research rationale. Later in 2007 Gavin Shatkin and I developed the first course in a long time to bridge architecture and urban planning in Michigan – Global Shelter Crisis – which is also an outcome of this research agenda. As a result of all this initiatives many term papers were written and parts of this research effort contributed to at least 5 doctoral dissertations that incorporated our research in various degrees. With their support we collected about one thousand plans, re-draw them all and applied a number of different calculations in order to assess their similarities and dissimilarities.

I am most grateful to this fantastic group of students and this book is dedicated to them. Youngchul Kim, Suma Pandhi, Romil Sheth, Omar Bahgdahdi, Stephanie Pilat, Kush Patel, Sara Blumenstein, Vera Baranova, Alingo Loh and Gavet Douangvichit in Michigan; Thais Biscaro and Estela Neto in Brazil.

Among the colleagues who inspired me and gave me invaluable insights and criticism are Robert Fishman and Harry Giles at Michigan, Rahul Merhotra at MIT, Juan Rois in Chicago/Rosario, Roger Hubeli and Julie Larsen in Urbana; Sonia Marques and Luiz Amorim in Brazil, Satoshi Nakamura in Japan and Anne Vernez-Moudon in Seattle. Doug Kelbaugh and Jean Wineman have also been very supportive at Michigan. Michael Benedikt and Lars Lerup met me only once in Ann Arbor when the Taubman College of Architecture was celebrating its centennial but their take on my research helped me immensely to re-frame the issue. As I prepare to move to their part of the world this book gives closure to the Global Apartments Research Group as it existed in Ann Arbor and open up new research possibilities for the work ahead in Austin.

Agradecimentos
tradução Elizabeth Martins

Este livro é o resultado de quase uma década de pesquisa sobre edifícios multi-familiares, mais conhecidos como apartamentos. Depois de ter defendido a minha tese de doutorado sobre a singular apropriação do modernismo no Brasil, eu retornei às minhas aulas em Belo Horizonte. Foi lá, no Programa de Pós-Graduação em Tratamento da Informação Espacial da PUC-Minas que esta pesquisa começou. A idéia original era a de utilizar as ferramentas de análise espacial para o entendimento da tipologia de habitação, ou o que o Professor João Francisco Abreu denominou de "geografia do domicilio". A utilização de dados do censo em ambiente GIS para o estudo das tipologias habitacionais possibilitou a conexão entre a minha formação em arquitetura e o meu trabalho de pós-graduação sobre a disseminação do modernismo, ampliando o alcance da minha investigação acadêmica, com o objetivo de fazer uma pesquisa mais generalizada e que produzisse dados mais confiáveis do que os usualmente encontrados nas pesquisas em arquitetura.

Foi na PUC-Minas, entre os anos de 2001 e 2002, que eu comecei a coletar plantas de apartamentos para a minha pesquisa. Em 2002, um financiamento do FIP (Fundo de Incentivo à Pesquisa), que me ajudou alavancar a pesquisa e galgar um projeto maior no CNPq, em 2003. Esta primeira coleta de dados me deu confiança para continuar e serviu para testar minha análise inicial, basicamente demonstrando que aqueles primeiros 200 apartamentos eram semelhantes ao ponto de terem quase que exatamente a mesma organização espacial.

Quando cheguei na Universidade de Michigan, em 2004, pensei em continuar com a pesquisa, mas não tinha uma idéia clara de como trabalhar com habitação no Brasil estando a 8000 kilômetros de distância. Mas assim que comecei a interagir com alunos de diferentes nacionalidades ficou claro que o que eu estava pesquisando não era uma tendência que ocorria apenas no Brasil, mas, sim, uma questão comúm a vários países. O interesse que os estudantes coreanos, indianos, russos e egípcios demonstraram durante os debates sobre o tema me incentivou a ampliar os raios da pesquisa ao nível global.

O Global Apartments Research Group surgiu da convergência de vários interesses. Eu queria aprender sobre apartamentos em diferentes partes do planeta e os alunos que vinham de diferentes países estavam empolgados por finalmente encontrarem um professor interessado no ambiente construído contemporaneo de seus países de origem. Durante quatro anos nos reunimos duas vezes ao mês durante o calendário acadêmico para discutir edifícios multi-familiares em 13 países diferentes (Brasil, Costa-Rica, India, Mexico, Egito, Finlândia, Itália, Coréia do Sul, Rússia, Alemanha, Estados Unidos, Turquia e Japão). Seminários de curta duração em Belo Horizonte (2006), Seoul (2007) e Natal (2007) me deram a oportunidade de aprimorar a nossa hipótese através de uma intensa imersão local.

Juntos aprendemos que os apartamentos são na realidade muito semelhantes, apesar de serem construídos em diferentes partes do mundo e de abrigarem famílias tão diversas quanto as brasileiras, egípcias e coreanas. Em 2006, uma bolsa do Office for the Vice President for Research (OVPR) da Universidade de Michigan possibilitou que eu organizasse a esses dados de uma forma ainda mais produtiva e promovesse o trabalho de alunos na análise de dados, alguns dos quais transformaram-se em capítulos para este livro. Durante este período, por duas vezes eu tive a oportunidade de oferecer um seminário sobre projetos de habitação, o que contribuiu para despertar o interesse dos alunos e consolidar os fundamentos da pesquisa. Mais tarde, em 2007, criei com Gavin Shatkin um curso que pela primeira vez em muitos anos integra arquitetura e planejamento urbano em Michigan. O curso Global Shelter Crisis também surgiu deste projeto de pesquisa.

Como resultado dessas iniciativas muitos trabalhos de final do curso foram elaborados e pelo menos 5 teses de doutorado incorporaram a nossa pesquisa de diversas maneiras. Com a ajuda dos alunos colecionamos mais ou menos 1000 plantas de apartamentos, redesenhamos todas e fizemos vários cálculos com o objetivo de avaliar as semelhanças e os contrastes. Também criamos um questionário que enviamos a 100 famílias no Brazil, na Rússia, Índia e na Coréia do Sul. Com base na análise quantitativa e no questionário criamos diversos diagramas em que dados coletados ganham forma visual.

Meus sinceros agradecimentos a este grupo fantástico de alunos, a quem dedico o meu livro. Em Michigan, Youngchul Kim, Suma Pandhi, Romil Sheth, Omar Baghdady, Stephanie Pilat, Kush Patel, Sara Blumenstein, Vera Baranova, Alingo Loh e Gavet Douangvichit; no Brasil, Thais Biscaro e Estela Neto.

Entre os colegas que me inspiraram e contribuíram com valiosas sugestões e críticas estão Robert Fishman e Harry Giles, da Universidade de Michigan, Rahul Merhotra, do MIT, Juan Rois em Chicago/Rosario, Roger Hubeli e Julie Larsen, em Urbana; Sonia Marques e Luiz Amorim no Brasil, Satoshi Nakamura no Japão e Anne Vernez-Moudon em Seattle. Embora eu tenha estado com Michael Benedikt e Lars Lerup uma única vez, por ocasião da comemoração do centenário do Taubman College of Architecture, na universidade de Michigan, os comentários que eles fizeram sobre a minha pesquisa me ajudaram muito na reestruturação da questão central. Em meio aos preparativos para a minha mudança para a terra deles, este livro encerra o Global Apartments Research Group de Ann Arbor e descortina novas possibilidades de trabalho em Austin.

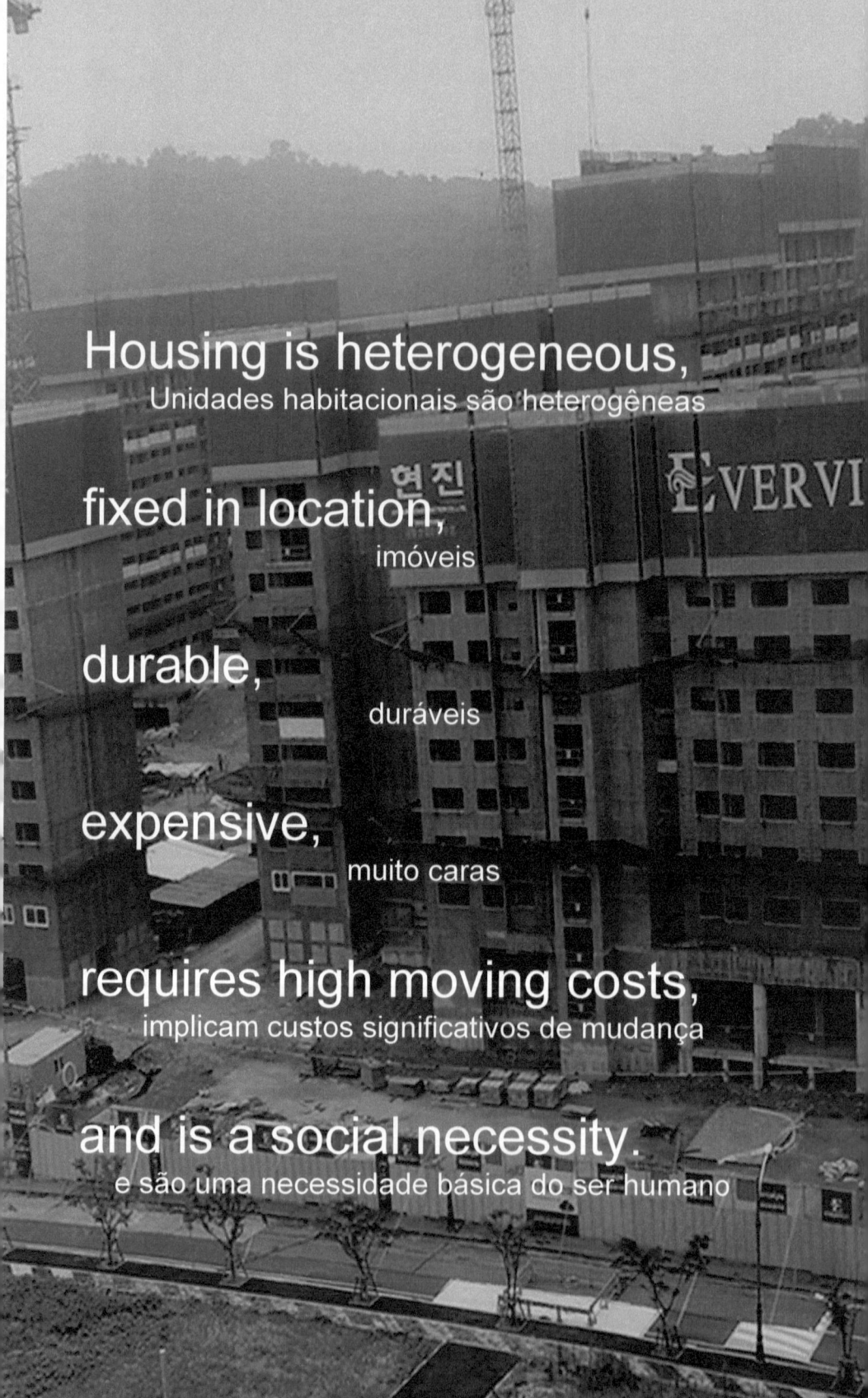

Housing is heterogeneous,
Unidades habitacionais são heterogêneas

fixed in location,
imóveis

durable,
duráveis

expensive,
muito caras

requires high moving costs,
implicam custos significativos de mudança

and is a social necessity.
e são uma necessidade básica do ser humano

Physical components are different. Locations are different. Because of these different settings, it is hard to substitute one house for another house.

Housing is fixed in a certain location. Because of this immobility, site characteristics affect housing characteristics.

In a neighborhood, activities of daily life are usually shared with neighbors, such as public school zones and community activities. In addition, each house can be categorized by its submarkets. These submarkets of location and neighborhood quality are hard to separate from the housing characteristics.

Once housing is built, it usually exists for decades, sometimes centuries. New housing supply is relatively small. Thus, most housing supply comes from existing housing stock. In addition, existing housing supply comes from property owners while new housing is supplied by builders and/or developers.

Housing price is many times larger than a household's annual income. In order to buy a house, people need to set up financial plans as well as to save money and manage their incomes.

Housing involves high transaction costs, which includes searching costs, legal and administration costs, adjustment costs, and financing costs. These transaction costs are different for owners and renters. Thus, residents need large amount of money for the moving costs as well as the housing price.

Housing is a basic necessity for people. Because it is a necessity, housing consumption is considered relatively price inelastic. In other words, it is hard to easily decrease or increase housing consumption in relation to the housing price.

Os componentes físicos de cada unidade habitacional são diferentes, assim como a localização. Por isso é uma unidade por outra. Unidades habitacionais são absolurtamente imóveis, não podem ser transportadas. Por causa desta imobilidade as características da vizinhança afetam a unidade habitacional.

Uma vez construídas as habitações geralmente duram muitas décadas, às vezes séculos. O número de novos domicílios é relativamente pequeno quando comparado com o total de unidades disponíveis.

O custo da habitação é normalmente muitas vezes maior do que a renda anual da família, demandando um planejamento financeiro de longo prazo. A compra de um imóvel envolve custos elevados de transação, que inclui a pesquisa, aspectos legais, comissões, custos administrativase custos do financiamento em si.

A habitação é uma necessidade básica para a espécia humana que não sobrevive muito bem no ambiente natural. Por ser uma necessidade, o mercado habitacional é considerado inelástico, ou seja, é difícil incentivar ou ou frear a demanda através de variações no preço.

Living differently in similar buildings.

Fernando Luiz Lara

As the 20th Century progressed, urban housing became quite homogenized throughout the world. Apartment buildings in Sao Paulo are very similar to those in Seoul, Moscow, and even Chicago. It is clear that the modernist architectural vocabulary made famous by the so-called "International style" has gone much beyond corporation identity buildings and prevails in the housing sector in most of the urbanized world. According to a study supported by the United Nations Habitat (ANGEL, 2000), residential buildings – although varying in size, shape and construction materials – now take on one of four basic forms: the single family house, the row house, the walk-up apartment building and the high-rise. This research project focuses on the three modern multi-family types, using the pre-modern typology of the detached house as a point of comparison when appropriate.

The main goal is to investigate the extent to which those buildings are or are not alike, or whether the similarities are more visual than experiential. The idea is that, although apparently related on the façade, more traditional ways of inhabiting still prevail in the way people appropriate these spaces. The main goal of this exploratory research is to investigate the means and the forms by which those modernist spaces (so comparable) are appropriated by local cultures (so diverse).

This research furthermore addresses the issue of how successful modernist architecture has been by becoming the predominant structure almost everywhere. Traces of the Dom-ino reinforced concrete proposal by Le Corbusier (1917) can be perceived in almost all residential buildings worldwide. This raises one simple, but rather provocative question: What if modernism had been more meaningful and had indeed appealed to a larger part of society? It is striking to perceive that the architectural literature of the 1970s and 1980s never pursued this question, assuming perhaps that modernism could never be popular (BROLIN, 1976; NEWMAN, 1980; VENTURI, 1966). Indeed, the development of modern architecture in the United States and in most of the Western World corroborates the idea that some of its intrinsic characteristics prevented modernism from becoming a popular success.

Modernism, however, has been much more popular than the traditional architecture historiography has portrayed. Once we go beyond formal characteristics so keen to architects, like proportions or choice of materials and start analyzing spatial relations and construction technologies and practices we might realize the extent to which our urban built environment has been homogenized (or not) during the 20th Century. And most of these constructive practices or spatial arrangements do come from the modernist experiments of the early 20th Century.

Existing literature reveals that "the spread of innovations resulted in the preponderance of similarities between cities across the globe: high-rise central business districts; suburbs and bedroom communities; transportation grids and limited access highways; urban renewal and redevelopment; international architectural styles..." (ANGEL, 2000, p.58). Twenty five years ago Frampton had already warned us that "the concept of a local or national culture is a paradoxical proposition not only because of the present obvious antithesis between rooted culture and universal civilization but also because all cultures, both ancient and modern, seem to have depended for their intrinsic development on a certain cross-fertilization with other cultures." (FRAMPTON, 1983: 314). Following Frampton's lead on the ancient roots of hybridist and exchange, this study focuses on the architectural styles of multi-family housing solutions, especially concerning spatial arrangements and the actual appropriation of those spaces.

Against the majority of the scholarly literature which focus, like Frampton did, on the dangerous or the dark side of globalization processes, this study takes a more optimistic approach to the housing homogeneity phenomena. While housing for the masses was just an utopian dream of avant-garde architects 100 years ago, construction on unprecedented scale throughout the world in the last few decades have led to an inevitable massification. Nevertheless, such massification have also led to a minimal quality standard for those able to afford it. Meanwhile, people have appropriated those similar units in quite different ways, a process of selecting which elements of modernity and which elements of tradition they want to adopt. The old aphorism think globally act locally can be translated into spread globally, appropriate locally.

The new technologies play a big role in the homogenized housing solutions, either with the use of the poured reinforced concrete system of slabs, beams and columns which have been adapted by every low-skilled construction industry in the developing countries or by the faster and more detailed processes of steel-structured buildings in the developed countries (as is the case of Korea in the 1990s). The discomfort with traditional styles is certainly one of the main reasons behind the modernist looks and spatiality. It is hypothesized that those countries were undergoing social, political and economic transformations for which modern architecture was a conveyor. It is also hypothesized that in the more developed countries where modernization was a presence and not a promise, the appeal of residential modern architecture has been smaller. The extent to which the spatial layout converge or diverge from mainstream modernism is one of the issues pertinent to the formal analysis component of this study. Another prominent component to be analyzed is the new programs introduced by the modern way of living. Some of the main questions asked pertain to which new spatial configurations were introduced and how people appropriated those spaces?

The literature on the apartment living in Brazil demonstrates that the process of verticalization started as early as the 1930s in Sao Paulo and Rio de Janeiro (VAZ, 2002) at first as a solution for the housing the working class but changed quickly to provide urban convenience to the upper-middle class. As a result, land prices soared in the inner areas of the major cities close to the center business districts in a process that has been expanding concentrically since the 1950s, housing more and more of the middle-class. At that time, the concentration of urban amenities and infrastructure in the center areas and inadequate mass transportation (by private or public means) kept the investment in high rises either in the city center or in its immediate vicinity. Later in the 1980s and 90s the economic stagnation and consequent increase in urban violence also contributed to transform the multi-family structures in virtual "vertical gated communities", spreading all around the city and often providing as many amenities as possible inside property lines.

As proven by the geographic diversity of papers in this edition, multi-family units are not unique to Brazil or to developing countries. Instead, it became a global phenomenon that has only escaped the anglo-axis. While suburbanization is the overwhelming reality of US,

Canada and Australia, the rest of the world has adopted multi-family arrangements as a solution to massive needs for housing. In the traditional European cities the multi-family has manifested itself in low rise (4-6 stories) buildings that predate the adoption of the elevator. Ironically, it was in Chicago that the machine to transport people vertically aka elevator turned pervasive, allowing us to build more in less land. The densification that followed took root in most cities around the globe, sheltering both office buildings and apartment units. But while the North-American society (with the exception of New York City) adopted multi-family downtown living only for your professionals and divorcees, pushing families to the suburbs, in the rest of the world families were attracted to centrally located apartments even after the automobile became pervasive in each country as the 20th century progressed. Another book would be necessary to explore the relationship between the highway system, urban renewal, the abandonment of inner cities and the North-American suburbanization. The interesting point to make is that despite being the focus of so much attention, sprawl is the exception and not the rule when we look globally.

One need only to browse satellite images made accessible by so many web-based mapping devices to see how much of the world is comprised of high-rise (above 5 stories) apartment buildings. When we started collecting plans we realized that they are indeed very similar, to the point of having almost always the same spatial structure. This generic spatial structure can be traced back to the early 20th century European Avant-garde but not much further back.

At the dawn of the 20th century each region of the world had a local housing typology. There was a Brazilian house type, a Korean house type, a Egyptian house type and a Indian house type. The pressures of urbanization on European cities at the second half of the 19th century created crowded slums that housed early industrial workers, while the wealth generated by the new processes built the first multi-family palaces of Paris and New York. As a housing solution, the apartments started both as housing for the very poor and the very rich. It was the European avant-garde of the 1920s that developed multi-family solutions into economic but healthy solutions that were supposed to house the working class. Units designed by J.P. Oud, Mies van der Rohe and Le Corbusier became classic and are still the reference today almost 100 years later.

When we look at the spatial arrangement of today's apartments it is striking to perceive the similarity with the avant-garde designs of the 1920s and 30s. A first and necessary step towards the understanding of this unique architectural phenomenon is the problematization of its significance vis-à-vis the context and the social and economical conditions in all those places.

For instance, when the Bauhaus was designing apartments to house the working class in the 1920s, the majority of the households were comprised of a family with children. Mom and Dad and two (or three, or four) kids were the norm and the units were designed for them. Nowadays architects still think of a family of four when designing apartments units but that arrangement is the absolute minority. In the USA only a little more than 30% of households are comprised of married parents with children. In Brazil more than half the households of the working class are multi-generation (grandparents at home) or female-headed. Are we designing for only 30% of the North-Americans and half the Brazilians?

Moreover, when we look at family routines it is clear that a South Korean family has a very different lifestyle when compared to an Indian or Egyptian household. Nevertheless, as this research shows, the apartments have almost always the same spatial arrangement. No wonder that when the condominium social contract collapses in low income housing projects the inhabitants take matters in their own hands and modify the spaces to meet their different demands as the work of Amorin and Loureiro has so well demonstrated in chapter 3. Given the urgent need for density and the unsustainable consequences of the single-family detached house for a planet approaching 7 billion people, we should be designing better apartments.

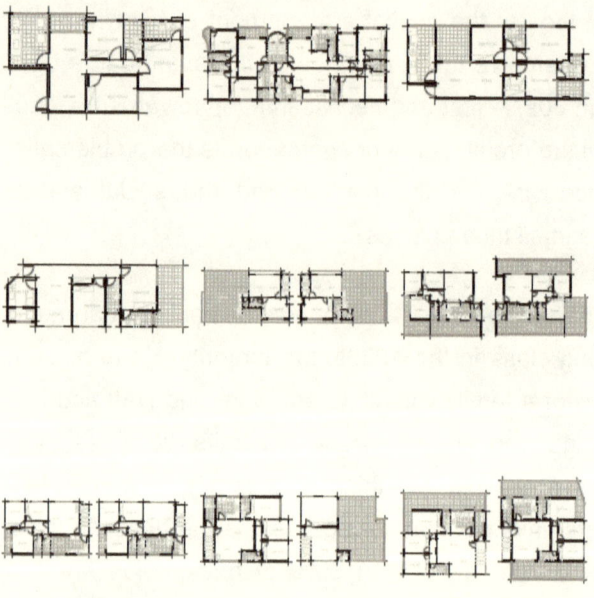

Vidas tão diferentes em espaços tão iguais

Fernando Luiz Lara, tradução Elizabeth Martins

Com o transcorrer do século XX, a habitação nas áreas urbanas se homogeneizou dramaticamente ao redor do mundo. Os edifícios residencias de São Paulo são muito semelhantes aos de Seul, Moscou e Chicago. Está claro que o vocabulário arquitetônico modernista que ficou conhecido pelo chamado "estilo internacional" disseminou-se para além dos edifícios corporativos e prevalece no setor imobiliário na maior parte do mundo. De acordo com um estudo apoiado pelo programa Habitat das Nações Unidas (ANGEL, 2000), os edifícios residenciais – embora variando quanto ao tamanho, a forma e o tipo de material usado na construção – tomam basicamente três formas: a casa unifamiliar, o sobrado, e os edifícios de apartamentos. Este projeto de pesquisa concentra-se nos três tipos modernos de edifícios multi-familiares, usando a tipologia pré-moderna da casa uni-familiar para fins de comparação, quando necessário.

O objetivo principal é o de investigar o grau de semelhança entre esses edifícios, ou se as semelhanças são mais visuais do que sensoriais. A idéia inicial é que embora as fachadas desses edifícios aparentem ser relacionadas, as práticas habitacionais mais tradicionais ainda prevalecem na maneira como as pessoas se apropriam desses espaços. O objetivo principal desta pesquisa exploratória é o de investigar os meios e as maneiras como esses espaços modernistas (tão semelhantes) são usados em diferentes culturas (tão diversas).

Além disso, esta pesquisa investiga a questão de quão bem sucedida a arquitetura modernista tem sido ao se tortnar estrutura predominate em quase todos os cantos do mundo. Traços do sistema Dom-Ino de Le Corbusier (1917) podem ser encontrados em quase todos os edifícios residenciais ao redor do mundo. Este fato levanta uma questão simples, mas muito estimulante: Como seria se o modernismo tivesse sido mais expressivo e com isso tivesse atraído uma fatia maior da sociedade? É surpreendente constatar que a literatura de arquitetura dos anos 70 e 80 nunca investigou a fundo essa questão, talvez por considerar que o modernismo não chegaria nunca a ser popular (BROLIN, 1976; NEWMAN, 1980). Na verdade, a evolução da arquitetura moderna nos Estados Unidos e na maior parte do mundo ocidental confirma a idéia de que algumas das características intrínsecas ao estilo impediram que o modernismo se tornasse um sucesso popular.

Entretanto o modernismo foi e ainda é muito mais popular do que a historiografia da arquitetura tradicional gosta de admitir. Uma vez que voltarmos a atenção para além das caracteristicas formais caras aos arquitetos, como proporçoes e materiais, e começarmos a analisar as relações espaciais e as tecnologias e práticas de construção, talvez possamos avaliar até que ponto o espaço urbano construído foi (ou não) homogeneizado ao longo do século XX. E a maioria dessas práticas de construção ou arranjos espaciais tem origem nos experimentos modernistas do século XX.

A literatura existente revela que "a expansão das inovações resultou na preponderância das semelhanças entre cidades ao redor do mundo: centros comerciais com edifícios altos; subúrbios e cidades dormitório; redes de transporte automotivo e estilos arquitetônicos internacionais …" (ANGEL, 2000, p.58). Há vinte e cinco anos Kenneth Frampton já havia alertado que "o conceito de uma cultural local ou nacional é uma proposta paradoxal, não somente por causa da antítese óbvia entre cultura enraizada e civilização universal, mas também porque todas as culturas, antigas e modernas, parecem ter precisado de uma certa influência de outras culturas para garantir o seu próprio desenvolvimento" (FRAMPTON, 1982: 314). Seguindo a percepção de

Frampton sobre as raízes antigas de intercâmbio e hibridismo, este estudo concentra-se nos estilos arquitetônicos que oferecem soluções para a habitação multi-familiar, especialmente no que se refere aos arranjos espaciais e à apropriação desses espaços.

Tomando o sentido contrário da literatura acadêmica que concentra-se, como no caso de Frampton, no lado negro do processo de globalização, este estudo faz uma análise mais positiva sobre o fenômeno da homogeneização da habitação. Enquanto no século passado um plano de habitação para as grandes massas era apenas uma utopia dos arquitetos de vanguarda, a escala acelerada e sem precedentes das construções ao redor do mundo nas últimas décadas resultou numa inevitável massificação. Todavia, essa massificação também resultou em critérios mínimos de qualidade para as pessoas com algum poder aquisitivo. Enquanto isso, as pessoas têm usado tais espaços semelhantes de maneiras bem diferentes, num processo de seleção entre os elementos tradicionais e modernos que desejam utilizar. O conhecido aforismo "pensamento global, ação local" pode ser traduzido como "disseminação global, apropriação local".

As novas tecnologias contribuem enormemente para as tipologias homogêneas de habitação, seja através do uso de colunas, vigas e lajes de concreto feitos no local e comumente usado pela vasta maioria da mão-de-obra não especializada do ramo da construção nos países em desenvolvimento, ou através dos processos mais detalhados e eficientes dos países desenvolvidos que utilizam os edifícios com estrutura de aço (como no caso da Coréia, na década de 90). O desconforto com os estilos tradicionais é certamente uma das principais razões por trás da aparência e espacialidade modernistas. Existe a hipótese de que esses países estavam atravessando transformações sociais, políticas e econômicas para as quais a arquitetura serviu de condutor. Existe, porém, outra hipótese com referência aos países desenvolvidos, onde a moderrnização já era realidade e não uma promessa, que considera que nesses países o interesse pela arquitetura residencial moderna não era tão grande. Até que ponto o layout espacial converge ou diverge do modernismo convencional é uma das questões pertinentes a este estudo. Outro componente importante a ser analisado diz respeito aos novos programas introduzidos pelo estilo de vida moderna. Algumas das nossas questões principais nos levam a indagar que novas configurações espaciais foram introduzidas e como as pessoas fazem uso desses espaços?

A literatura sobre edifícios residenciais no Brasil demonstra que o processo de verticalização começou na década de 1930 em São Paulo e no Rio de Janeiro (VAZ 2002), inicialmente como uma opção de moradia para a classe trabalhadora, e que rapidamente se transformou em uma solução de conveniência para a classe média alta. Como consequência, os preços dos terrenos dispararam nas áreas próximas dos centros comerciais das grandes cidades num processo que vem se expandindo em anéis concêntricos desde a década de 1950, abrigando mais e mais moradores da classe média. Naquela época, a infraestrutura e a rede de serviços urbanos estavam concentrados nos centros das cidades e o transporte de massa inadequado (tanto o público quanto o privado) colaborou para manter o interesse dos compradores nos edifícios altos na parte central das cidades ou nos bairros próximos ao centro. Mais tarde, nas décadas de 1980 e 1990 a estagnação econômica e o consequente aumento da violência urbana também contribuíram para transformar as estruturas multi-familiares numa espécie de "condomínios verticais fechados", espalhados práticamente por toda cidade e, no geral, oferecendo o maior número possível de serviços e opções de lazer dentro dos limites do condomínio.

Como podemos comprovar pela diversidade geográfica dos textos contidos neste livro, os edifícios multi-familiares não são uma característica peculiar do Brasil ou de países em desenvolvimento. Na verdade, os apartamentos tornaram-se um fenômeno global que só não prevalece no eixo anglo-saxão. Enquanto a suburbanização é uma realidade predominante nos Estados Unidos, Canadá e Austrália, o resto do mundo adotou o os arranjos multi-familiares como solução para a enorme demanda habitacional.

Através do uso de imagens de satélites que podem ser facilmente acessadas pela internet podemos constatar a enorme quantidade de edifícios com mais de cinco andares espalhados pelo mundo. Quando começamos a colecionar plantas de apartamentos percebemos que eles eram muito semelhantes, ao ponto de terem quase exatamente a mesma estrutra especial. Esta estrutura especial genérica existe desde o começo do século XX na Europa quando foi elaborada pelas vanguardas modernas.

Poderíamos então afirmar que há 100 anos cada região do mundo tinha a sua tipologia de habitação local. Havia uma tipologia brasileira, uma tipologia coreana, uma tipologia egípcia e uma tipologia indiana. A crescente urbanização da Europa na segunda metade do século XIX resultou no surgimento de áreas densamente povoadas onde moravam os trabalhadores das indústrias, enquanto que a riqueza produzida pelos novos processos construía os primeiros palácios multi-familiares de Paris e Nova Iorque. Como solução habitacional, os apartamentos foram construídos primeiro para os muito pobres e para os muito ricos. Foram as vanguardas européias da década de 1920 que criaram soluções multi-familiares econômicas e saudáveis destinadas à classe trabalhadora. Unidades projetadas por J.P. Oud, Mies van der Rohe e Le Corbusier tornaram-se clássicas e ainda são referências nos dias de hoje, quase cem anos depois.

Quando analisamos os arranjos espaciais dos apartamentos de hoje em dia é surpreendente perceber a semelhança com os desenhos das décadas de 1920 e 1930. Um primeiro e necessário passo para a compreensão deste fenômeno contemporâneo da homogeneização é a problematizção de sua significância vis-a-vis o contexto e as condições sociais e econômicas em todos esses lugares.

Por exemplo, quando Bauhaus estava projetando apartamentos para a classe trabalhadora na década de 1920, a maioria dos lares era composta de famílias com filhos. Arranjos domésticos de mãe, pai e dois (três ou quatro) filhos representavam o padrão e as unidades foram desenhadas para eles. Atualmente arquitetos ainda pensam nas famílias de quatro pessoas quando desenham unidades de apartamentos, mas esse arranjo representa a absoluta minoria. Nos Estados Unidos, somente 32% dos lares são compostos de casais com filhos. No Brasil, mais de metade dos lares da classe trabalhadora são compostos de pessoas de diferentes gerações (por exemplo, com avós morando na casa) ou de mulheres chefes de família. Estariam os arquitetos projetando para somente um terço dos americanos e metade dos brasileiros?

Além do mais, quando analisamos as rotinas familiares fica claro que a família sul coreana tem um estilo de vida muito diferente dos indianos ou egípcios. Entretanto, como demonstra esta pesquisa, os apartamentos apresentam o mesmo arranjo espacial. Não chega a surpreender que quando o contrato social do condomínio em projetos de habitação para pessoas de baixa renda entra em colapso os moradores ignoram as regras e modificam os espaços de acordo com suas necessidades, como demonstram Amorin e Loureiro no capítulo 3. Enquanto o capítulo 2 explica a metodologia adotada os capítulos 5 a 10 investigam a homogeneização em escala global, de João Pessoa na Paraíba a Seoul na Coréia, passando pelo Cairo, Moscou, Tokyo e pelos conjuntos para baixa renda norte-americanos.

Devido à necessidade urgente de sustentabilidade e as consequências insustentáveis das habitações uni-familiares para um planeta com quase 7 bilhões de habitantes, nós deveríamos estar desenhando apartamentos melhores.

REFERENCES:

ALTHEIDE, David & JOHNSON, John, "Criteria for Assessing Interpretive Validity in Qualitative Research", Chapter 30 in Handbook of Qualitative Research, edited by Denzin and Lincoln, Thousand Oaks: Sage Pub, 1994.

ANGEL, Shlomo. Housing Policy Matters: a global analysis. New York: Oxford U Press, 2000.

BROLIN, B., "The Cultural Roots of Modern Architecture", The Failure of Modern Architecture (New York: Van Nostrand, 1976).

BONDUKI, Nabil, Origens da Habitação Social no Brasil, São Paulo: Estação liberdade: Fapesp, 1998, 342pp.

COLOMINA, Beatriz, Privacy and Publicity, Cambridge: MIT Press, 1996.

COLOMINA, Beatriz. "Collaborations: the private life of modern architecture", Journal of the Society of Architecture Historians, September 1999, pp. 462-471.

CORBUSIER, L. Towards a New Architecture (1923), New York: Dover Pub., 1986, pp.289.

CUNNINGHAM, Allen, Modern Movement Heritage, London: E&FN Spon,1998.

DEVLIN, Kimberly & NASAR, Jack. "The beauty and the beast: some preliminary comparisons of "high" versus "popular" residential architecture and public versus architects judgment of same", Journal of Environmental Psychology vol. 9, London: Academic Press, 1989, p.333-344.

FRAMPTON, Kenneth. Modern Architecture: A Critical History (New York: Oxford U Press, 1982).

GARCIA-CANCLINI, Nestor, Hybrid Cultures: Strategies for Entering and Leaving Modernity, Minneapolis: U of Minnesota Press,1995.

HILL, Jonathan, Occupying Architecture: between the architect and the user, London: Routledge,1998.

HUYSSEN, Andreas. After the Great Divide: Modernism, Mass culture, Post-modernism, Bloomington: Indiana U Press, 1986.

LARA, Fernando. "Brazilian Popular Modernism: analyzing the dissemination of architectural vocabulary", forthcoming on the Journal of Architectural and Planning Research, 2005.

LARA, Fernando. "Designed Memories, the roots of Brazilian modernism", in Memory and Architecture, edited by Eleni Bastea, Albuquerque: U of New Mexico Press, 2004, pp.79-98.

LARA, Fernando. "One step back for two steps forward: the maneuverings of the Brazilian avant-garde" Journal of Architectural Education, 55/4, May 2002.

NASAR, Jack. "Urban Design Aesthetics: The evaluative qualities of building exteriors" Environment and Behavior, 26/3, May 1994, Sage Publications, 1994, p. 377-401.

NEWMAN, O., "Whose Failure Is Modern Architecture?" in B. Mikellides (ed.) Architecture for People (New York: Holt, Rinehart and Winston, 1980) pp. 45-58.

PUTNAM, Tim. "The modern home and the evolution of the house", The Journal of Architecture, vol 9, winter 2004, pp. 419-429.

ROWE, Peter. "Modern Housing on the Rise, 1920-1930" in Modernity and Housing, Cambridge, MA: MIT Press, 1993, pp.74-.102.

SMITH, Elizabeth A. T. (editor), Blueprints for modern living: history and legacy of the Case Study Houses, Cambridge: MIT Press, 1998, 256pp.

UN-HABITAT. The Challenge of Slums: a global report on human settlements, London: Earthscan Publications, 2003, pp. xxv-xxxiv and 1-55.

ZEVI, Bruno. The modern language of architecture, Seattle: University of Washington Press, 1978.

VAZ, Lilian. Modernidade e Moradia: habitação coletiva no Rio de Janeiro, séculos XIX e XX. Rio de Janeiro: 7Letras, 2002

Methodology

Fernando Luiz Lara

Our Global Apartments Research Group at the University of Michigan's Taubman College of Architecture has been systematically collecting data on apartments across the globe. With the help of international graduate students, we have compiled an inventory of hundreds of apartments plans, from the 1920s European avant-garde and other paradigmatic 20th century designs, all the way to buildings being marketed nowadays in Brazil, India, Russia, Egypt and Korea.

In the past five years we have collected a sample of about 200 contemporary apartments from cities as diverse as São Paulo and Belo Horizonte in Brazil, Cairo in Egypt, Moscow in Russia, Mumbai in India, and Seoul, Korea.

Our data collection departs from selecting plans of current buildings from publicity folders or web-based advertisement to be analyzed in the following manner: The plans are re-drawn in Auto-Cad for accuracy and brought to scale using doors as dimensional reference (when no dimensions are given or the scale is misleading). A series of area calculations are performed, this information is coded into an spreadsheet and used to compare for instance the proportion of areas devoted to social, private or service-oriented functions. A simple space-syntax calculation of "mean depth" (how far the spaces are, in average, from the entry door) is performed, an acronym for privacy. Later on, the plans are then analyzed in terms of integration and visual connectivity, using space-syntax software Depth-Map.

The area calculations allowed us to perform a number of cross-country comparisons. The analysis includes calculations of each apartment's total square footage, including area calculations of social space (dining, living and family room), service space (kitchen, bath and laundry), private space (bedrooms), circulation space, and veranda/porch/balcony space.

In addition to area calculations, each apartment's spatial depth is computed. The spatial depth is a concept developed by Space Syntax theories and determined by the number of rooms through which one must traverse in order to reach a particular space. For example, if one must travel through 2 spaces in order to arrive at a particular room, that room has a spatial depth of 3 (an additional point is included for the room itself). The final spatial depth is the average of all the spatial depth values in the floor plan. Using the average numbers from different sets of apartments allow us to infer similarities and differences between countries. For instance, Brazilian apartments have the largest portion of area devoted to services (kitchen, laundry, maid's room), almost the same share of space (25%) used for social activities(living room, dining room),   while in Indian apartments the same social area takes 40% of the total. Korean apartments on the other hand devote in average 20% of the total area to verandas, a calculation that supports the tacit knowledge about Korean's obsession with southern (sunny) orientation.

The depth calculations allowed us to check various degrees of privacy (the deeper the unit the more privacy layers it supposedly have). In our sample, the Korean apartments were slightly more private-oriented than the Brazilian ones (3.8 vs 3.4 mean depth) but the Indian apartments were really outliers with an average of only 2.3 and such less private-oriented spatiality combined with the largest portion of area devoted to private areas (40%) will be discussed better in the chapter by Romil Sheth. The Indian apartments are also outliers in terms of depth versus area calculations. Units usually become more compartmentalized and therefore "deeper" as the total area increase but in our sample from Bombay the opposite happened, apartments became "shallower" as they grew in size.

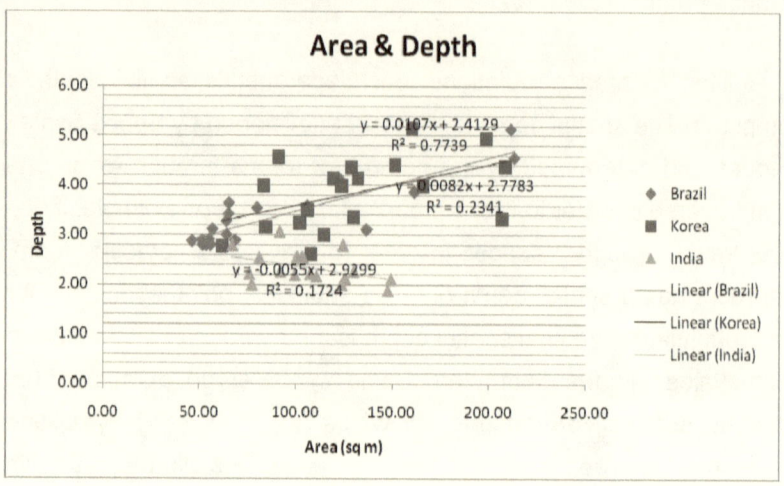

We are aware of the arbitrariness of our choices and the fact that our sample might not be exactly representative given the small number of cases compared to the size of the construction markets in the respective countries. But when thinking about our sample with a qualitative perspective, it is clear that after looking at 20 to 25 plans we reach a point of saturation after which no new information (or in our case spatial arrangement) is provided by adding more plans to our analysis.

As a way to effectively compare apartments from different countries we are developed a dissimilarity index. The first version of the index is shown in the graph below. Individual apartments are plotted according to their level of integration or segregation (calculated as space syntax mean depth) and affordability (as a ratio of consumer price divided by median income).

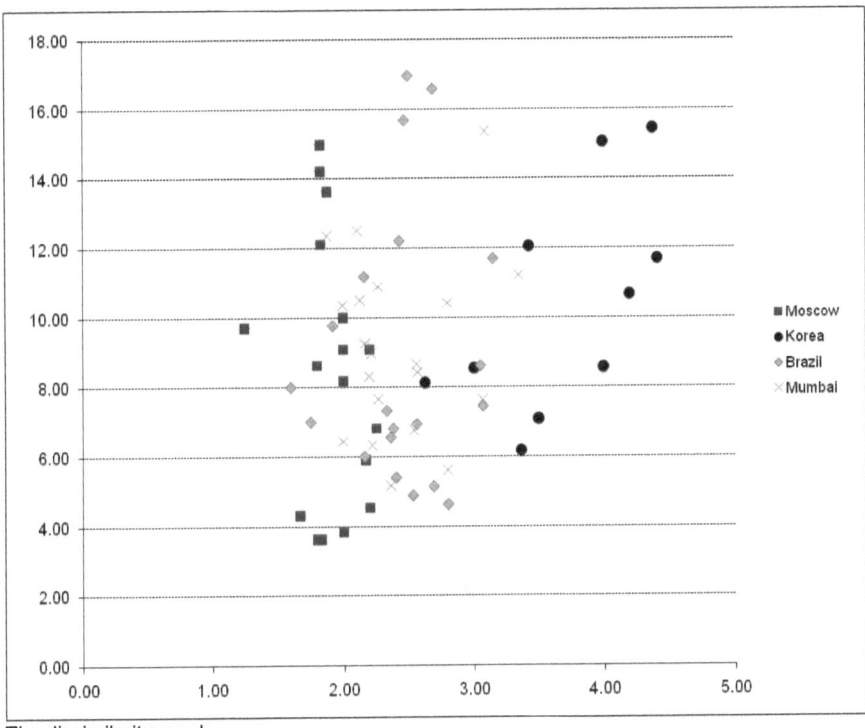

The dissimilarity graph

THE QUESTIONNAIRES

But we are also very much interested in the fact that no matter how similar are the apartments, different people will always inhabit them in slightly different ways. In order to investigate the validity of the above statement and learn more about how people appropriate their apartments, we developed a questionnaire that was sent to about 20 households in each of four countries: Brazil, Korea, India and Russia.

In the questionnaire people were asked to sketch a plan of their apartment and provide information about how many people live in the unit, their age and sex. IN addition, they were asked to tell us where in the household each member spends time in a regular day, in 15 minutes intervals.

In order to maximize the response rate of this pilot survey, we used a snow ball technique of distribution in which a number of questionnaires were sent to acquaintances in the three countries and they were asked to pass it along to other acquaintances living in apartments. No other information that would identify the respondent was collected and the return envelope had no name or address. We also understand that the sample is quite small and not statistically significant nor representative. Nevertheless, we learned so much from the 70 returned questionnaires that we were compelled to make the results public here.

For instance, it was striking to perceive that 50 min per day is the average time that a Korean family interacts in the same space. This data is not statistically representative but we believe that the real number is not very different. The questionnaire basically asked people to register in which room (bedroom, living, kitchen, etc.) each member of the family normally is, in intervals of 15 minutes throughout the day. Actually, the questionnaire does not ask if the family is really interacting (they can all be in the same room immersed in individual activities) but assumes that in order to interact people need to be in the same space. In any case, it is frightful to perceive that we are becoming more and more isolated from one another, a trend that is evident when see each member of the family with his/her own bedroom, own bathroom, own car and watching their own TV or using their own computer (which in our questionnaire would count as interaction if people are at the same space).

But the fact that bedrooms are proportionally larger in Brazil was quite a surprise, as well as the result from the questionnaires that Brazilians are spending more time in their bedrooms then the Koreans. The Brazilians love to think of themselves as very outgoing social-oriented people and everyone of us who spends some time abroad complain about how much we miss our social activities. But here is the trick, when we asked people in Brazil and in Korea to tell us how much time they spend in the social areas of their apartments (living room, dining room, varandas) versus private areas (bedrooms), the Koreans are spending 76% more time in the social quarters (3hs21min for the Koreans, 2hs31min for the Brazilians).

One can say yes Brazilians are more social outside of home but how to explain the fact that Brazilians spend more time in their bedrooms (9hs21min) than the Koreans (9hs05min). Or do the private life in the apartments do not provide an accurate account of our contemporary life-style?

We also found striking gender differences in the use of space. In all four countries mothers spend in average more time in the kitchen than all other family members combined. Supporting the idea of very traditional gender roles in India, out of 19 questionnaires, not a single male was reported spending any time in the kitchen.

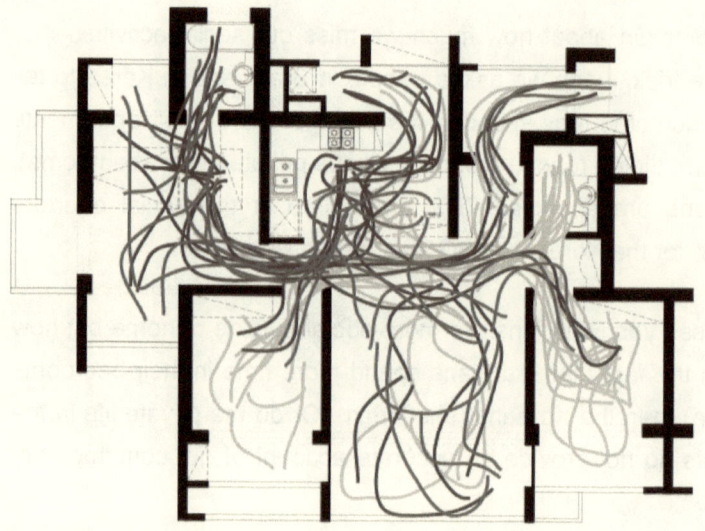

daily movement of a family

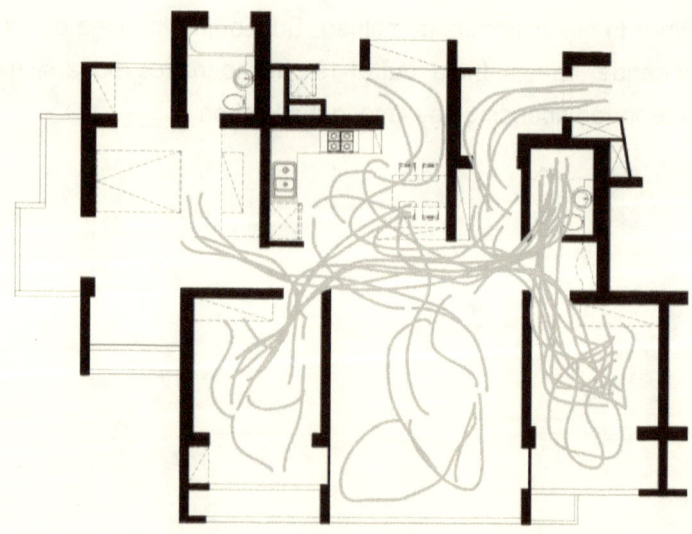

daily movement of the mother only

Metodologia

O grupo de pesquisa Global Apartments sediado entre 2005 e 2009 no Taubman College of Architecture da Universidade de Michigan, EUA, tem sistematicamente coletado plantas de apartamentos de diversas cidades ao redor do mundo. Com a ajuda de alunos de graduação e pós-graduação oriundos de diferentes países, foi montada uma base de dados com centenas de apartamentos que vão desde as vanguardas Européias dos anos 1920 até unidades sendo vendidas em 2009 no Brasil, na Índia, na Rússia, no Egito e na Coréia do Sul.

A coleta de dados parte de uma seleção de apartamentos a partir de folders publicitários ou anúncios na internet. As plantas dos apartamentos são re-desenhadas em CAD e trazidas para a escala correta, muitas vezes utilizando-se de artifícios como as dimensões das portas ou de outros equipamentos, na ausência de medidas nas plantas originais. Uma série de cálculos de área são feitos para que seja possível comparar por exemplo o tamanho das áreas privativas (quartos) com as áreas de serviço ou sociais. Estas informações são organizadas numa planilha e depois consolidadas para comparações diversas intra ou extra países. Um cálculo simples de "profundidade" é feito para comparações básicas de níveis de privacidade. Profundidade é um termo emprestado das análises de sintaxe espacial que funciona como parâmetro para graus de privacidade, quanto mais profundo (mais espaços precisam ser cruzados para se chegar ao objetivo) mais privativo. Algumas das plantas foram também analisadas de forma mais detalhada com o uso de softwares como Depth-Map desenvolvido pela equipe do University College London.

Os cálculos de área nos permitem inferir algumas diferenças (ou semelhanças) entre os países pesquisados. Os apartamentos brasileiros por exemplo têm a maior parcela de área devotada aos serviços (cozinha, lavanderia, quarto de empregada), quase a mesma proporção (25%) usada para atividades sociais (sala de estar e jantar), enquanto nos apartamentos indianos a mesma área social chega a 40% do total. Os apartamentos da Coréia do sul por sua vez apresentam varandas que ocupam em média 20% da área total, um número que suporta a observação de que os coreanos são obcsecados com as varandas e sua orientação para o sul.

Os cálculos de profundidade nos permitem verificar graus de privacidade (quanto mais profundo mais privativo). A profundidade espacial é um conceito desenvolvido por teorias da Sintaxe Espacial e determinada pelo número de espaços que se atravessa para alcançar um espaço em particular. Por exemplo, se é necessário passar por 2 espaços a fim chegar em um quarto, esse quarto tem uma profundidade espacial de 3 (um ponto adicional é incluído para o próprio quarto). A profundidade média é dada pela soma de todos os divido pelo número total de espaços da unidade. Usando tais médias podemos fazer várias comparações entre países. Em nossa amostra, os apartamentos coreanos eram ligeiramente mais privativos que os brasileiros (3.8 e 3.4 de profundidade média) mas os apartamentos indianos se revelaram bastante diferentes com apenas 2.3 de profundidade média.

Cientes da arbitrariedade das nossas escolhas e do fato de que nosso universo é muito pequeno quando comparado com o número de unidades habitacionais em cada cidade ou mais ainda país, ressaltamos que de maneira alguma nossa coleta pretende ser representativa e correta estatisticamente. Mesmo assim, dada a baixíssima variação na organização espacial dos apartamentos contemporâneos pelo mundo a fora, fica claro que a partir de 20 ou 25 plantas coletadas em um determinado país chega-se a um ponto de saturação a partir do qual qualquer outra unidade acrescentada dificilmente traz uma informação nova.

Como forma de efetivamente comparar apartamentos de diferentes países nós desenvolvemos um Índice de Dissimilaridade (ver figura na pag 35). Cada uma das unidades analisadas é plotada no gráfico usando-se como eixo horizontal a média da profundidade (quanto menor o número menos privativo ou mais integrado é a unidade) e como eixo vertical uma medida de custo relativo em que o preço da unidade é dividido pela renda média familiar (o resultado seria o tempo, em anos, que uma família deveria trabalhar para poder comprar tal unidade).

Além disso, nossa pesquisa também se debruçou sobre o fato de que apesar das unidades habitacionais serem muito parecidas, famílias em diferentes partes do planeta ainda mantém modos de vida diversos. Para avaliar a validade da afirmação acima nós desenvolvemos um questionário que foi enviado para 20 domicílios em cada um dos seguintes países: Brasil, Coréia do Sul, Índia e Rússia. O questionário solicitava ao morador que esboçasse a planta do apartamento e nos informasse sobre a idade e o sexo de cada um dos moradores. Em seguida, foi pedido aos moradores que preenchesse uma tabela nos dizendo em qual espaço cada um dos moradores estaria, em intervalos de 15 minutos, em um dia comum. Para maximizar o número de respostas ao questionário nós usamos uma técnica de bola-de-neve em que vários questionários foram enviados para pessoas do nosso conhecimento para que fossem repassados a vizinhos e outros conhecidos. Desta maneira conseguimos uma resposta de quase 90% com 71 dos 80 questionários devolvidos e corretamente preenchidos. Apesar das limitações estatísticas e da não-representatividade, os resultados foram tão interessantes que resolvemos torná-los públicos aqui.

Por exemplo, foi impressionante perceber que 50 minutos por dia é o tempo médio que uma família coreana passa junta no mesmo espaço. Estes dados não são estatisticamente representantivos mas acreditamos que o número real não seja muito diferente. Pior ainda, o questionário não pergunta se as pessoas estão realmente interagindo (podem todas estar no mesmo quarto dedicadas a atividades individuais) mas supõe que a fim interagir as pessoas necessariamente devem estar no mesmo espaço. Em todo o caso, é duro perceber que estamos nos tornando cada vez mais isolados uns dos outros, uma tendência que fica evidente quando se vê cada membro da família com seu próprio quarto, seu próprio banheiro, sua própria televisão e seu próprio laptop.

Mas o fato que os quartos são proporcionalmente maiores no Brasil foi também uma surpresa, assim como o resultado de os brasileiros estão passando mais tempo nos quartos do que os coreanos. Enquanto brasileiros adoram se dizer sociáveis, quando pedimos que famílias no Brasil e na Coreia nos dissessem quanto tempo gastam nas áreas sociais de seus apartamentos os coreanos revelaram passar 76% mais tempo ali. (3hs21min para os coreanos, 2hs31min para os brasileiros). A hipótese de que o brasileiro passa mais tempo se socializando fora de casa também caiu por terra no nosso questionário dado que o tempo gasto nos respectivos quartos (9hs21min) foi maior do que na Coréia (9hs05min).

Nós encontramos também impressionantes diferenças de gênero no uso do espaço. Em todos os quatro países as mães gastam na média mais tempo na cozinha do que todos outros familiares somados. Reforçando a permanencia desses valores tradicionais no uso do

espaço os questionários da Índia não registraram um único homem
adulto passando míseros 15 minutos na cozinha.

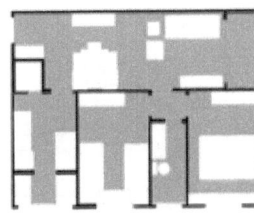

apartment redrawn

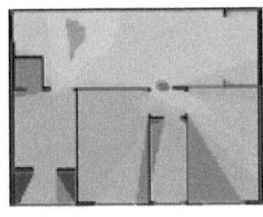

space syntax analysis

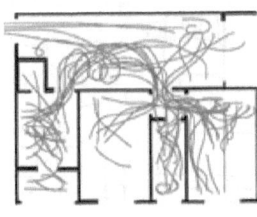

movement diagram

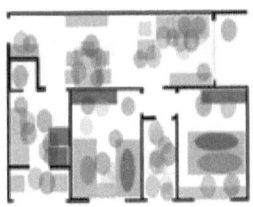

permanence diagram

Can a fig tree bud roses?
Studying spatial transformations in public housing.

Luiz Manuel do Eirado Amorim e Claudia Loureiro
translated by Alida Perrini

Conheci Luiz Amorim e Claudia Loureiro há uma década atrás quando ainda cursava o doutorado e comecei a participar de conferências acadêmicas no Brasil. Confesso que fiquei encantado desde o início com a forma brilhante com que juntavam indagações teóricas e análises empíricas em suas pesquisas. Junto com Sonia Marques, outra pernambucana genial, Amorim e Claudia são minha principal referência em qualidade de pesquisa em Arquitetura no Brasil.

"Uma Figueira pode dar Rosas?" é um texto clássico desta postura que mistura observação do espaço construído brasileiro e análise sofisticada para responder a perguntas insistentes da disciplina da Arquitetura, no caso como funcionam a longo prazo os apartamentos para famílias de baixa renda.

Amorim e Loureiro fazem uma detalhada análise de todas as transformações encontradas em conjuntos habitacionais no Recife e suas implicações da sintaxe espacial. Como o texto em português está disponível em (http://www.vitruvius.com.br/arquitextos/arq000/esp053.asp) optou-se por privilegiar a publicação da versão em inglês completa.

The correspondence between the Portuguese poetess Florbela Espanca and her editor, Professor Guido Batelli, inspired the title of this paper. According to the poetess, the education she was brought up could not be blamed for what she has called "her character's defect", because she was exactly what she ever was. Further, she suggests that there are "impossible transformations: a fig tree cannot bud roses" (cf. Dal Farra, 1996). What Florbela highlights is the perpetuity of some facts, i.e., the impossibility of some kinds of change in nature. This calls our attention to an urban phenomena which, silently, has been changing dramatically the housing estates built by the Companhia de Habitação do Estado de Pernambuco – COHAB-PE, along Recife's metropolitan region. Because these housing estates are freed from urban regulations, they have been trans formed into an unpredictable and indescribable object. They challenge the current professional taxonomy, which aims at describing and classifying urban arrangements and building types. This paper addresses these changes by observing, from a typological point of view, the housing units and the urban setting. It also discusses the need for a new taxonomy to answer the question: are fig trees budding roses?

CREATING FORM: Project norms and rules, codes and conventions

The creation of form highlights two aspects. On the one hand, a set of norms and rules, functioning as design instruments, brings about ideas that order form and organize space. On the other hand, codes and conventions of use redefine the form created by a project, along with the organization of uses and activities. Between these two poles, there is congruence and confluence. In other words, a traditional standpoint searches for the harmony found in that which serves the purpose for which it was made, translating timeless qualities which form the way to operate and to come into being; on the other hand, confluence reveals an experimental vision – unexpected and unplanned qualities that inform the moment (Johnson, 1994). The organization of domestic space is part of this bi-faceted process of form creation, in which, if on the one hand the professional viewpoint orients itself through precise and harmonic taxonomies, then on the other, a daily viewpoint creates a new agenda to be attended to.

Houses, whether detached, terraced, single or multi-storied, are generally characterized by direct access between the public and private domains. Conversely, apartment buildings are characterized by the aggregation of housing units into communal units that share common spaces, principally those intended for accessing the public domain. The composition of such housing units utilizes geometric rules that define the field of possibilities of form aggregation in order to meet the objectives of sheltering domestic activities. These laws also establish possible manners of adapting the spatial arrangement, such that the theoretical nature of such delimitation provides for a certain predictability of transformations, always according to the same laws.

It is curious to observe that, in this aspect, the changes that occur in the housing estates located in the periphery of Recife, particularly in apartment buildings, seem to attempt to overcome such geometric restrictions. Virtually no building remains restricted to the original structure, with successive extensions in all directions. In order to carry out such transformations, the occupants completely subvert the rationality imposed by economic restrictions for the construction of large scale housing complexes. They introduce concrete structures without acknowledging the established resistance for the original structure, they freely modify supporting walls, and they erect extensions without observing retreats between buildings or between buildings and the street.

44

Formally, the transformations are rather significant. Openings do not follow the patterns imposed by the project; the occupants expand verandas, balconies, closets and flower boxes; they introduce new coverings and utilize new sidings. Of these transformations, the one that seems most significant is the one that goes least noticed alongside the exuberance of the geometric and constructive modifications. It refers to its generating principle: the search for a direct access from the street to the housing unit, in other words, a negation of the condominium principle and a return to the public-private relation present in a house. This desire is so strong that the search for direct access to the street can be found on all floors, from the ground floor to the higher floors. Always possible by the transgression of collective rules.

These transformations are also perceptible in the configuration of public spaces: whether they were originally designated for access, circulation, or leisure, they are universally privatized by the expansion of housing units and by the construction of trade and services equipment. The occupants transform the original pattern, based on the displacement of parallel buildings inside open urban blocks into a succession of patios, alleys, and passages, creating a special configuration which resembles spontaneous settlements, given the creation of new configurational relations (Figure 1). Curiously, transformations in public spaces seem to follow a path that is exactly opposite to that found in the housing units. If in the housing units there is an attempt to overcome the geometric restrictions that characterize the phenomenon of transforming apartment buildings, in the public spaces it is precisely the small number of such restrictions, or their apparent absence that allows a greater liberty of transformation of the urban space – in other words, here occupants overcome the absence of rules. In a certain sense, one can affirm that occupying public spaces and modifying the buildings are two aspects of the same phenomenon. The more conspicuous aspect is the one that redefines geometric limits, subverts the constructive and projective rationality, and seeks to establish new rules of accessibility in the system. The less visible aspect is the one that redefines codes of use that are essentially codes for social life and spatial life.

WAYS OF LIVING: From houses (multi or single family) to apartment buildings

Modern apartment buildings – complexes of juxtaposed residential units, served by spaces for common use – seem to have appeared in the city of Recife in the 1930s. But this form of juxtaposed multi-family habitation is not new. In fact, old multi-level houses from colonial times known as *sobrados* had already been converted from single-family homes to separated units, one family on each floor, served by a shared stairway. This conversion points to a process of substitution of habitants – the better-off classes transfer themselves to the suburbs, which causes the spatial restructuring of colonial units in the central areas of the city. Originally meant for the occupation of only one family, as explained by the French engineer-architect Vauthier in his records about eighteenth century Recife, multi-storied houses came to constitute condominium units with families occupying individual stories. The spatial structure itself of such multi-storied houses facilitated such an occupation, because, generally speaking, the floor plans of the various levels were exactly the same, to the surprise of many outsiders and visitors (Vauthier 1975).

That the form of the urban sobrado remained for the construction and elaboration of living space was fundamental for the emergence of a housing transition type, found in various central neighborhoods of the city as early as the 1930s, in which the multi-leveled type establishes the general rules for the spatial structuring and functional organization of small multi-family buildings. These transitional units are terraced buildings, varying from three to five stories, with the ground level (sometimes with a mezzanine) being occupied by commercial activities, and the rest used for living spaces, directly accessible from the street by a side stairway (Amorim & Loureiro, 2000).

These forms of multi-family habitation, sharing the same roof and property, answered the growing demand for middle-class housing in the city. In that vein, it is the private and public insurance companies that are responsible for introducing to the city a new type of housing organization for the working middle-class, adopting modernist principles. For example, the Institute of Retirement and Pensions for Industry Workers (IAPI – Instituto de Aposentadoria e Pensões dos Industriários) built an innovative apartment building, designed by the architect Carlos Frederico Ferreira, in 1939, composed of duplex housing units, a rare solution even today (Silva, 1988:23).

Until the 1970s, however, multi-family solutions in any form did not apply to housing for lower income populations in Recife – for this segment, the standard was detached housing units on individual plots grouped together in housing estates. This was the predominating solution since the emergence of the Social League Against Mocambos,1 an eradication program implemented by the state government between 1939 and 1945. The goal of the program was to substitute mocambos, which in 1938 represented nearly 60% of housing in the city, with more adequate housing units: hygienic, comfortable, and durable. The exception to the detached houses pattern is seen in a single housing complex constructed under the

---

1 *Mocambo* literally means hut, and originally referred to runaway slave communities in rural Brazil. Since the early twentieth century, it has come to refer to slums around cities like Recife.

command of the League. Meant for trade workers, it was composed of joined buildings with two stories, one residential unit on each story, each with independent access. Only at the end of the 1970s is the solution of the apartment building applied to public housing estates, built by the Housing Company of the State of Pernambuco (COHAB) in Cohab Rio Doce 4. In the housing estate, groups of buildings on pilotis are arranged in urban blocks without individualized lots, whose urban design is based on the same modernist principles that shaped the Brasilia's superquadras2: the ground floor is open, public, democratic, thereby establishing a tenuous gradation between the public and private domains, expressed by the absence of control gates, except for the access hall to the apartment buildings.

The use of pilotis in this housing estate, however, constitutes a unique experience – in the examples that follow it, the pilotis are eliminated and the area is occupied by apartments. However, the urban design concept remains, displacing apartment buildings within open public spaces. They are largely three or four storey high, in double bar form, interconnected by buildings' vertical and horizontal circulation systems. In each estate, this type of structure is combined with single-family homes – beyond the open blocks of apartment buildings, isolated houses, single-storied or double-storied, terraced or not, they are arranged in traditional blocks, with plots of approximately 200 square meters.

What distinguishes the two solutions, houses and apartments, among other characteristics, is the pattern of access to the residential unit – while in apartments, street access is from a common, shared space, in houses, it is independent and exclusive to the occupant. In apartment buildings, halls, access stairways, and landings constitute ambiguous zones between the interior and the exterior of the residence and their use is regulated by judicial, physical, and behavioral codes. In houses, the ambiguity is eliminated by a gate that separates the plot from the street, playing the role of a threshold. Another distinctive trait is the open, public and uncontrolled space of the ground floor that surrounds the apartment buildings– its classification is ambiguous, without defined front, back, or sides. In houses, the retreating space is private and controlled, separated from the public domain by a wall, a physical and legal barrier that classifies the portions of the plot – front, back and sides are clearly defined. In a house, In a house, the resident has determining power over the use of this space – the front and back yards have purposes that see to the interests of the family. In blocks, the use of the remaining space is an object of negotiation, it should see to the needs of not one but various families, besides the community that lives in the neighboring area. It is, in fact, not an extension of the home, but of the street. The following chart summarizes the differences.

Variables	House	Apartment Building
Access (in relation to the street)	Private – single Direct and independent	Public Indirect and shared
Space beyond the house	Private – extension of the house	Public – extension of the street
Use of the plot	Meets the needs of the family	Meets the needs of the community
Symbolic nature	Individual	Communal
Geometric opposition (in relation to the street)	Next to – public Remote – intimate	Next to – public Near – public Remote – intimate
Topological opposition (in relation to the street)	Front – public Back – intimate	Front/back - public

FROM APARTMENTS TO ISOLATED HOUSES

After some decades of occupation, the profile of these complexes housing estates is distant from its original conceptions. Supposedly unrealizable transformations result in the definition of a new project (in the sense of a projection of the interests of the residents) and the generation of new codes and uses. The variants of the transformations are innumerous. What they have in common is the fact that, more than a new project, new limits are established, or definitions between public vs. private, front vs. back, above vs. below, inside vs. outside. Subjacent to the diversity of the identified formal expressions, could a new architectural type be generating itself? Describing some of the typical occurrences could help comprehend this uncharted phenomenon.

 One of the most common modifications that occurs in the apartments on the ground floor is the addition of a terrace to the side wall of the building, connecting the living room directly to the exterior, to a "front" garden, obtained by walling in the public retreat space, which is sometimes occupied by a garage. The entrance of the apartment is moved from the common corridor located between the two parallel blocks to their sides. This simple reform has two consequences – one refers to the new convention of use and the other to a new geometric rule: with the inversion of the entrance, the occupant removes himself from the

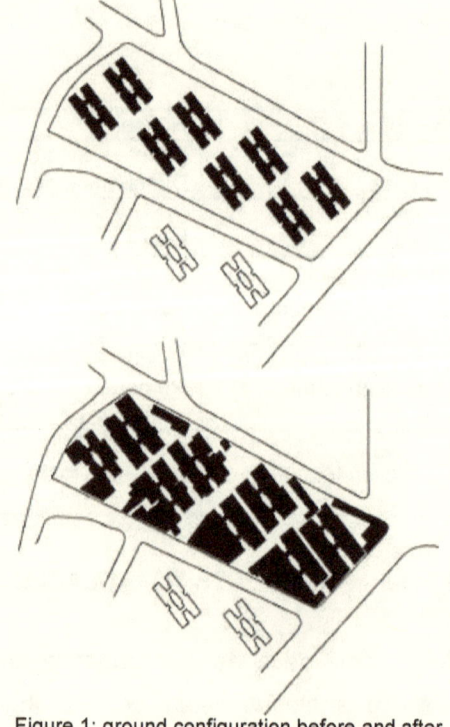

Figure 1: ground configuration before and after

collective obligations having to do with the common areas; second floor occupants can then also expand their apartment on top of the flagstone that is added for the terrace. From there, yet another possibility arises: with their apartment already expanded beyond the limits of the outer walls, the second floor occupant adds an outer stair, thereby taking advantage of the same convention of use as their downstairs neighbor. Two apartments, then, are converted into two isolated homes, juxtaposed, with independent access. If the urban block is located on a higher plain than the public road, the areas resulting from the level difference of the plains lower than the building can be incorporated in the formation of units in two or three floors, housing a garage and spaces for trade or services (see figure 4).

However, transformations don't always follow this path of from the ground up. From the second or third floor, a structure sent into the retreat space of the street serves as a base for the expansion of an apartment. Or even, the expansion of the ground floor is part of the second floor apartment reform, transforming them in a duplex. Or the process can be intercalated or alternated. Or even, an extreme variant of the process is the occupation of the roof of the building for the private use of the occupants of the top floor.

On the other hand, symbolic expressions of individuality deconstruct the principle of compositional harmony and constructive rationality. The windows of the new expansions do not follow the model of the original building, neither from the dimensional, modular, or typological point of view. Each one establishes their own standard, possibly seeing to their taste, to their need for individuality or to budget restrictions: in this way, Venetian windows, arched windows, diverse types of window grates, flower boxes, diverse types of siding, provide the complex with a final aspect that is far from the monotony that comes from the repetition of the same elements. Less radical transformations consist of opening of windows on blind edges of the building: a search for new views, better orientation, or internal rearrangement?

Figure 1 shows a block from the COHAB Curado 3 complex, built in the Metropolitan Region of Recife (RMR), in the municipality of Jaboatão dos Guararapes.   It is located on an uneven relief at a peripheral location on the side of a federal road, near an industrial district. This complex, like other estates built in the RMR, was built in stages – the first two stages (Curado I and II) are composed of two to three-room detached houses. In the other stages, the urban designers adopted a mixture of housing types – apartment buildings and single-family houses.

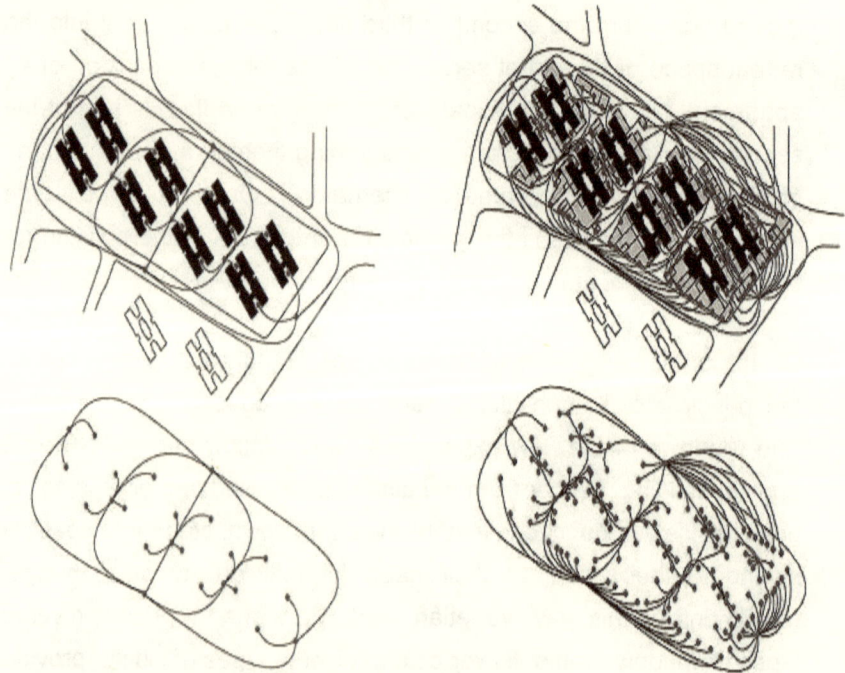

Figures 2 and 3 – mapping original and current configuration

The compositional principle of the multi-family buildings consists of the repetition of the same element: a double-barred block in the shape of an H. These are arranged according to the appropriate orientation, parallel to the longer side of the urban quarter. Minimal access control and little differentiation of the polarity between public and private define the interstitial spaces. Figure 1 also shows the current situation of the block: the residents occupy or reclaim the interstitial spaces for private use, accentuate the differentiation between free spaces through the formation of allies, passages, and ways, and differentiate pedestrian movement between the interior and the exterior of the block.

This process of gradual appropriation of the free spaces in the block redefines the interface between the public and private domains. Figures 2 and 3 show maps of these interfaces for the situation of the project and for the current situation. In the original composition there are few points at all – whether they are indicative of an open space with an entrance or of an interface. In the current situation, these points multiply themselves, forming an intricate web of local and global relations, similar to that found in urban tissue of spontaneous growth.

UNDERSTANDING THE REMODELING

One way to understand the effects of the remodeling that occurred in the open spaces referred to in the previous section, is by describing their accessibility properties before and after being remodeled. The effect of these transformations can be observed graphically by the representation of all the possible lines of visibility and accessibility in two instances: as they were conceived by the architects and as they were modified by the occupants. In order to allow for a quantitative evaluation, these lines are presented in a gradation of colors, representing the average distance of each line to all the others. This means to say that the darker lines are the most accessible and the lighter the most remote.

The designed spatial system provides some interesting properties. The first is the existence of lines of circulation that intensely cross the block's interior. Second, it is precisely these lines that are the shortest in the whole system, which means to say that there is a rather large possibility that these lines correspond to the lines of the most pedestrian movement in the block (Hillier et al., 1993). The modified system, in its turn, demonstrates an absolutely different configuration from the one previously observed. The lines of greatest access (dark) are found in the periphery of the block, suggesting that movement would occur in great intensity in the paths surrounding the block. The paths thereby guarantee a gradient of privacy between the more public spaces and the more private ones – between the residing community and the rest of the block.

What one can deduce from this simple analysis of the syntactic properties of the two systems is that the modifications introduced by the population in a random manner generated a spatial system that seeks to avoid the internal use of the block on the part of the population of the complex. That given, it is possible to restitute some properties that seem to be absent in the designed spatial system. Firstly, a certain gradient of privacy. Second, the reestablishment of a kind of logic in the existing polarities in the traditional urban structure – relation between closed and public spaces, expressed by the duality of front/back. By defining a hierarchical system of movement, the occupants establish more clearly a separation between that which is public – the access paths of the complex, and that which is private,

54

the inside of the block. In this manner, even without being able to invert the polarity of front and back, a relation of public and private substitutes it: though not necessarily from the back of the block, spaces that are more private achieve access to the apartments.

However, it is noted that in the diverse remodelings found in the COHAB Curado 3, there are significant cases in which occupants seek to restore the sense of frontality in their housing units by constructing independent stairs of direct access from the public way. In this manner, they restore the relation between closed and opened space, alongside the structure of traditional settlements. The multiplication of direct access points between the street and the new building units when compared to the original system also points to this, as seen in Figures 4 and 5.

In a certain sense, the modifications in the morphology of the block are oriented in a mode that gives the ordered urban form, which is composed of the same closed elements systematically repeated in a monotonous rhythmic compositional pattern (full/empty), a more structured urban form in which a random aggregation of non-modular units substitutes the logic of the repetition of modulated units, in the sense of creating more evident local differentiations and generating a more diverse global system. On a scale of values that are understood between order and structure, the housing estates studied slowly migrate from one extreme to the other, distancing themselves from the formal predictability of the modernist model, and approaching the unpredictability and apparent disorder of spontaneous settlements.

A FIG TREE THAT BUDS ROSES

The design of the analyzed complexes is based on the concepts of *Existenzminimum*, a set of basic needs that would guarantee a minimum level of dignified living for any citizen – universal needs. The realized transformations infer another level of necessities, requirements just as indispensable as a roof to live under, air, light and minimum services. These would be related to the binary oppositions that organize the use of domestic space, as Lawrence (1997) points out: masculine vs. feminine, right vs. left, front vs. back, clean vs. dirty, symbolic vs. profane. Research by diverse authors suggests how important it is for the resident to have the possibility of partitioning spaces and zones that permit the expression of these binary codes in the ordering of domestic activities. The expression of these binary codes is at once functional, spatial, social and psychological – their classification is as much demarcation as the transfer between any of the poles of the code (cf. Lawrence, 1977). In this manner, where, how, why, and when this transfer processes itself is a question of the project: how public becomes private, front becomes back, profane becomes symbolic. The question is translated by the identification of implicit codes and conventions by opposing explicit norms and rules, as Lawrence (1997) points out, which define limits of the project and of the use of domestic space, notably, transition spaces and limitation between domains.

The observed transformations are recurring, and happen in practically all of the housing estates in the periphery of Recife. They point to different conceptions of the binary codes mentioned above. These differences present themselves in the initial consideration of the project, for the professional that designs it and the resident who uses it. Alongside these different conceptions is the understanding of two spatial properties and their relations with social attributes that regulate the use of space – accessibility vs. co-presence and visibility vs. co-awereness. Better put, it refers to the control that is exerted over the accessibility – which separates or selectively reunites others, and over visibility – related to the possibility of being aware of significant others. According to Hillier & Hanson (1984), use and movement create standards patterns of spatial life, in other words, a potential encounter field and co-presence, which are systematic relationships and a by-product of the spatial design. Such relations resulting from the project are more global, a field of movement and co-presence that involves strangers passersby. The intervention of the residents, in its turn, creates more local relationships, among inhabitants. The intervention of the residents, in its turn, creates more local relationships, among others that are nearer. All the same, one can affirm that the expectations of the project and the expectations of the residents in terms of the use of space are extremely opposed to that which Holanda defined as a paradigm of formality and a paradigm of urbanity (Holanda, 1997).

The different expectations can be illustrated by a recent journalistic work about the transformations that occurred in housing units. Recently, two apartment buildings in Olinda, metropolitan region of Recife, that had collapsed with fatal consequences called media attention to the phenomenon of the transformations here described and the subject came to be amply discussed. It is curious to note that in the referred report, the interviewed professionals (architects and engineers) commented on the transformations from the point of view of the transgression of a certain aesthetic and constructive order established by formal knowledge. At no point did these professionals observe the reasons for which the residents modified the originally conceived object, nor the consequences, from the point of view of use, of the apparently disordered actions. The report established a necessity to control the transformations because they had been done without adequate technical aide, putting its own residents at risk.

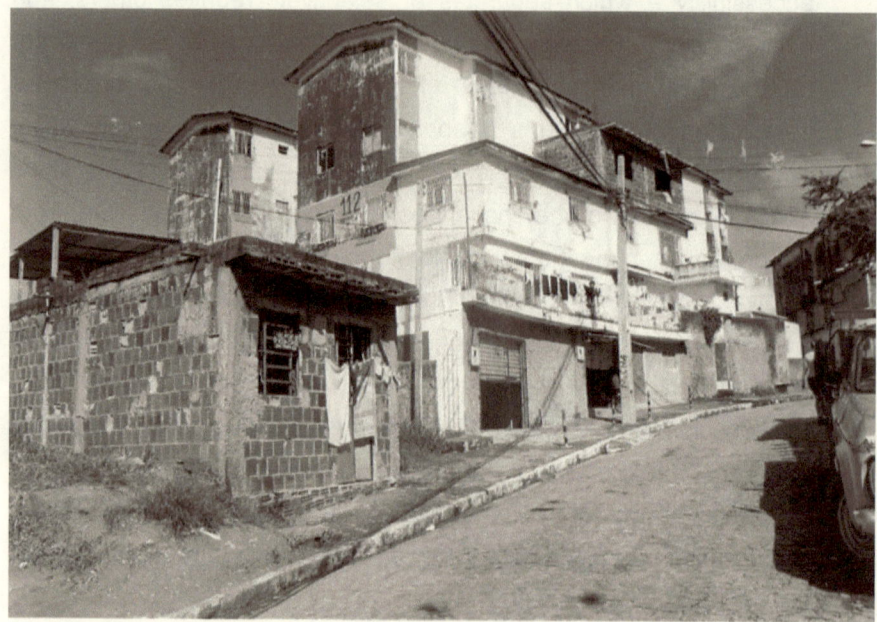

Figure 4: View of the the Curado Complex with added structures

The phenomenon summarily discussed in this article presents other facets that need particular investigation. If many times the key to the understanding of certain phenomena is in their irregularity, then the preservation of original characteristics of certain complexes or of building types constitutes an object of fundamental study for the understanding of the process of remodeling in its totality. Researchers observed, for example, that the building constructed on pilotis presented a low index of transformation, the ground floor being largely empty or occupied by garages. Why isn't the pilotis occupied, if the situation of an independent structure and a completed and covered floor seems more proper for occupation? In the case of the complex where the pilotis solution was adopted, the transformations manifested themselves in the sense of delimiting the building lot, by subdividing the block. Development studies intend to explore these other forms and hope that some of the answers found here will make possible a reformulation of the critical discourse regarding the disordered process of occupation of the free spaces in popular complexes of the region, demonstrating that this phenomenon originates in the social housing program's inadequacy and in their design proposal.

REFERENCES:

AMORIM, L. & LOUREIRO, C. O Morar Coletivo. Recife: Relatório de Pesquisa DAU/UFPE/Laboratório de Projeto, 2000.

DAL FARRA, Maria Lúcia. "Florbela: um caso feminino e poético". In: Espanca, Florbela. Poemas de Florbela Espanca. São Paulo: Martins Fontes, 1996.

DALTON, Nick. SpaceBox software. London: University College London, 1993.

HILLIER, B. et al. Natural movement: configuration and attraction in urban pedestrian movement. Environment and planning B: planning and design. London, Vol. 14, 393-385, 1993.

HILLIER, B. & HANSON, J. The social logic of space. Cambridge: Cambridge University Press, 1984.

HOLANDA, F. d. Exceptional space. Ph.D. thesis submitted to the Bartlett School of Graduate Studies; University College London; University of London, 1997.

JOHNSON, Paul-Alan. The theory of architecture: concepts, themes, & practices. New York: Van Nostrand Reinhold, 1994.

LAWRENCE, Roderick J. "Public collective and private space: a study of urban housing in Switzerland". In: KENT, Susan (ed.). Domestic architecture and the use of space: an interdisciplinary cross-cultural study. Cambridge: Cambridge University Press, 1997, pp 73.

MONTEIRO, Circe. A sala invisível: análise da vivência domiciliar estendida em conjuntos habitacionais. Recife: Relatório de Pesquisa. DAU/UFPE/Laboratório de Projeto, 2000.

SILVA, Geraldo Gomes da. "Marcos da arquitetura moderna em Pernambuco". In: SEGAWA, Hugo. Arquiteturas no Brasil/anos 80. São Paulo: Projeto, 1988.

VAUTHIER, L. L. "Casas de residência no Brasil". In: Arquitetura Civil I. São Paulo: FAU-USP/MEC-IPHAN, 1975. pp. 1-94.

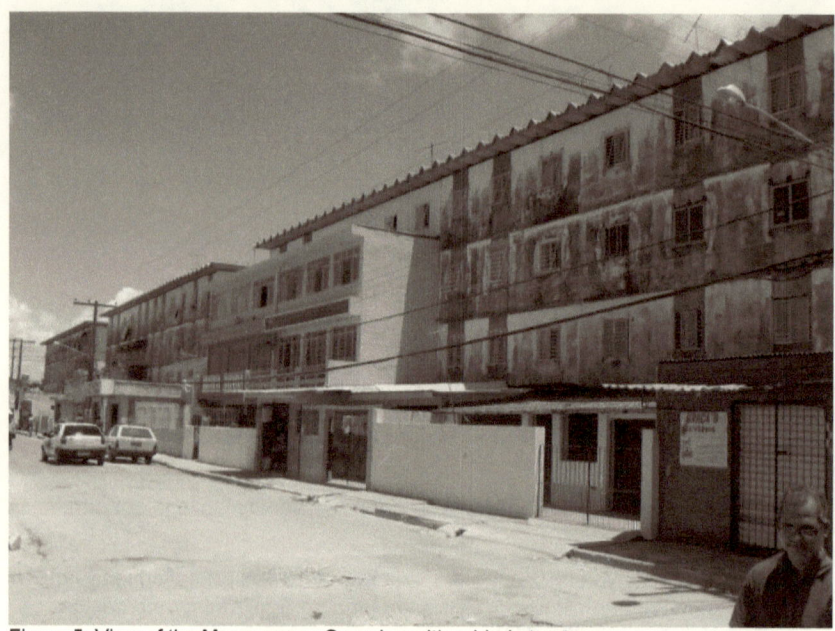

Figure 5: View of the Maranguape Complex with added structures

A Moradia na Alemanha e no Brasil: os exemplos de Freiburg i.B. e Florianópolis/SC.

Adriana Gondran Carvalho da Silva

Among the many good research published in Vitrivius, the leading Brazilian online architectural journal, one called my attention a few years ago: a piece comparing apartments in Florianópolis in Brazil with Freiburg, Germany. Adriana Silva, the author, is finishing her PhD at the University of Weimar and this paper, originally written as a class assignment, fits so well our conversations at the Global Apartments Research Group that we thought we needed to include it here. The original text can be found online at (http://www.vitruvius.com.br/arquitextos/arq000/esp420.asp).and here we have a summary of the ideas.

Moradia, habitação, casa, domicílio ou espaço doméstico são os nomes dados ao lugar onde o ser humano vive. Este espaço não serve apenas como proteção, por exemplo, contra as turbulências da natureza, do clima, e de animais selvagens, mas também contra o próprio homem.

Estilos de vida, gostos e personalidades moldam as formas, funções e estética das habitações – mas os modos e cultura do morar correspondem também às normas da sociedade, aos materiais à disposição e às fontes culturais (1).

As transformações das moradias e das edificações remetem assim a transformações da sociedade, dos casais e das famílias, da divisão social do trabalho e relações de dominação, comportamentos sexuais e características de personalidade. Deste modo, Häußermann e Siebel afirmam que: "através das transformações das plantas baixas das moradias pode-se decifrar as transformações no morar" (2).

O objetivo desta pesquisa é apontar para algumas das diferenças entre as moradias alemãs e brasileiras, considerando-as como reflexos das diferenças culturais entre as duas sociedades. Para tanto, primeiramente investigou-se a história da casa na Alemanha e no Brasil e o significado de seus ambientes, agrupados em três categorias: o setor social, o setor íntimo e o setor de serviços. Em seguida, foram analisadas duas plantas baixas de moradias, localizadas nas cidades de Freiburg i.B. e Florianópolis/SC. Estas cidades foram escolhidas porque apresentam imagens em nível nacional semelhantes, consideradas ícones de qualidade de vida e que atraem anualmente milhares de novos habitantes.

As plantas baixas estudadas correspondem a apartamentos com área interna de aproximadamente 110 m2, destinados a famílias compostas por 4 a 5 pessoas (casal e 2 ou 3 filhos) com perfis econômicos análogos. A seleção dos apartamentos foi feita através de buscas em sites da internet, de maneira a aproximar este trabalho à realidade do mercado imobiliário, que não apenas responde a questões econômicas, como também a sociais e culturais.

É necessário ainda salientar que fatores demais condicionantes, tais como fatores climáticos, técnicas e materiais de construção, implantação no sítio, orientação solar, volumetria e fachadas das edificações não foram considerados neste trabalho. Trata-se de um estudo comparativo empírico e bidimensional, baseado em observações cotidianas.

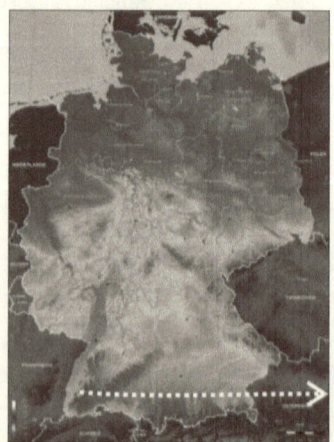
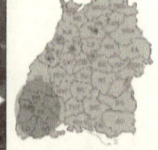

Alemanha   **Freiburg i.B.**

O EXEMPLO ALEMÃO

O primeiro apartamento localiza-se na cidade de Freiburg im Breisgau, situada no sudoeste da Alemanha, entre a Floresta Negra, a Suíça e a Alsácia. É também a maior e mais ensolarada cidade da região e atrai anualmente um grande número de turistas e de estudantes internacionais. É famosa por sua qualidade de vida e equipamentos urbanos. (3). Freiburg i.B. é também conhecida como a capital ecológica e "Solar-City" da Alemanha e do mundo. Estar no meio da natureza, foi e é o objetivo dos seus cidadãos, protegendo o meio ambiente para assim assegurar o futuro. Os objetivos da política ambiental da cidade correspondem a esta atitude, que é a base para o seu eficaz e persistente desenvolvimento (4). O bairro em que se situa este apartamento (5) é uma área residencial com boa infra-estrutura, onde jardins-de-infância, escolas e lojas são facilmente alcançados a pé. Com os equipamentos de lazer do Lago Dietenbach, tem-se à disposição um verdadeiro parque para relaxamento e bem-estar.

A planta baixa do exemplo alemão é basicamente composta pelos seguintes ambientes e circulação, perfazendo aproximadamente 110m2:

Setor Social: hall, sala de estar/jantar;
Setor Íntimo: três dormitórios, duas sacadas e banheiro compartimentado;
Setor de Serviços: armário e cozinha.

A tabela 01 indica as áreas de cada setor e em relação à área total do apartamento:

Setor	Área (m2)	Percentual
Setor Social	24,00	21,80%
Setor Íntimo	54,50	49,60%
Setor de Serviços	13,00	11,80%
Circulação	18,50	16,80%
Total	110,00	100,00%

Tabela 01: Quadro de Áreas do Apartamento de Freiburg i.B.

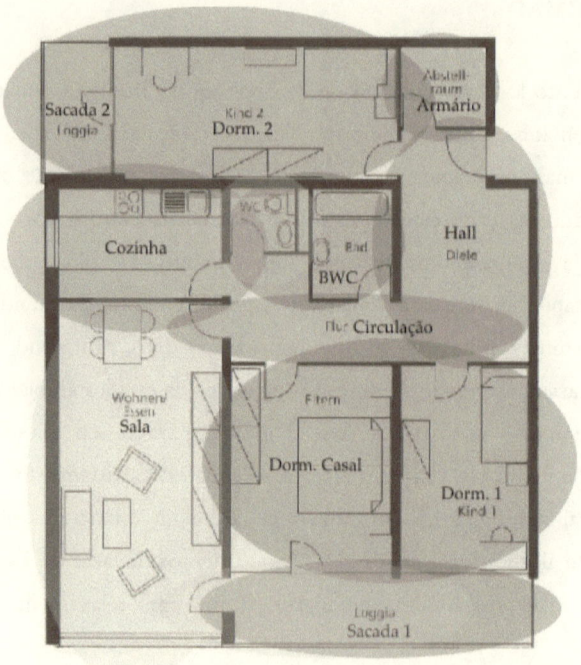

Setor Social ■ Setor Íntimo ■ Setor de Serviços ■ Circulação
Planta Baixa do Apartamento de Freiburg i.B.
Fonte: ImmobilienScout24, 2006

Uma das características mais significativas do apartamento de Freiburg i.B. é a superposição entre seus setores social e íntimo, observadas nos usos comuns da sacada 1 – pelos dormitórios e sala – e no banheiro compartimentado. Outra é clara definição espacial da circulação, que permite a ligação entre todos os ambientes, sem criar zonas de transição ou hierarquias.

A falta de hierarquização é também visível entre os dormitórios: não há grandes variações nas dimensões, formas, ou acessos. A própria sala de estar/jantar, considerada como o ambiente maior e melhor decorado pela Norma DIN 18011 (6), não tem possui qualidades arquitetônicas que o diferenciem, sendo tratado como mais um quarto (ein Zimmer).

O EXEMPLO BRASILEIRO

O segundo apartamento localiza-se na cidade de Florianópolis/SC, situada na região Sul do Brasil (27° de latitude), parcialmente no continente, parcialmente na Ilha de Santa Catarina. Desde 1950, o município tem como base econômica a atividade turística. Sua imagem de "capital com a melhor qualidade de vida do país" tem atraído, todos os anos, uma grande quantidade de novos habitantes, impulsionando assim o mercado imobiliário.

O bairro em que se situa este apartamento fica nas proximidades da Universidade Federal de Santa Catarina e da Lagoa da Conceição. Devido ao seu caráter exclusivamente residencial, não possui estabelecimentos comerciais ou de serviços, e o perfil econômico dos seus moradores é de classe média e alta.

A planta baixa do exemplo brasileiro é composta pelos seguintes ambientes e circulação, perfazendo aproximadamente 110m2:

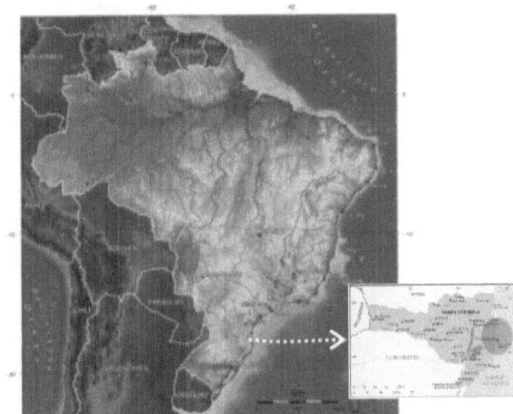

Brasil   **Florianópolis**

Setor Social: hall, sala de estar/jantar e sacada;
Setor Íntimo: dois dormitórios, um banheiro, uma suíte com closet e sacada;
Setor de Serviços: cozinha; área de serviço, banheiro de serviço e quarto reversível/dependência de empregada.

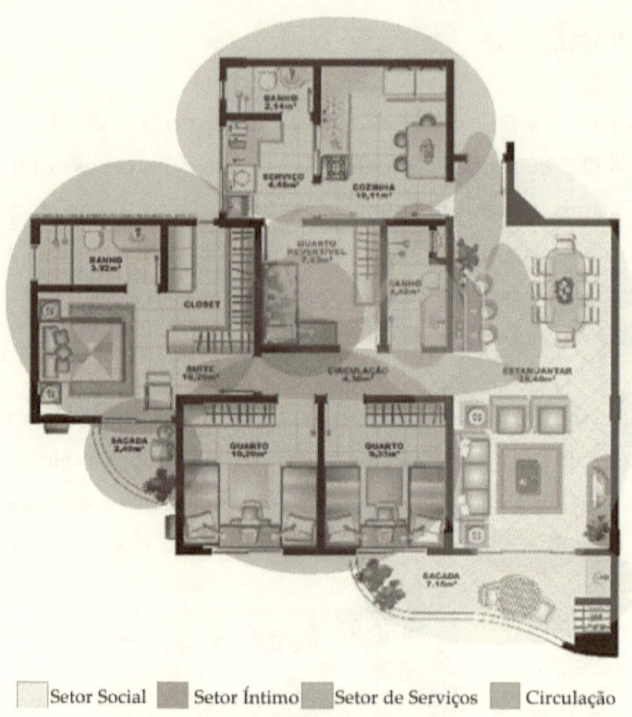

Setor Social ☐ Setor Íntimo ■ Setor de Serviços ■ Circulação ■

Planta Baixa do Apartamento de Florianópolis/SC
Fonte: Hantei Engenharia, 2006

A tabela 02 indica as áreas de cada setor e em relação à área total do apartamento:

Setor	Área (m2)	Percentual
Setor Social	35,40	32,20%
Setor Íntimo	46,00	41,80%
Setor de Serviços	24,20	22,00%
Circulação	4,40	4,00%
Total	110,00	100,00%

Tabela 02: Quadro de Áreas do Apartamento de Florianópolis/SC

A principal característica da planta baixa do apartamento de Florianópolis é a superposição de usos entre os todos os seus setores: o banheiro íntimo é também social e o quarto reversível pode servir como dependência de empregada, mais um dormitório ou como escritório (Home Office).

A circulação é bem definida no setor íntimo, entretanto é dependente dos demais ambientes para acessar o exterior, o que produz zonas de transição e dificulta a disposição do mobiliário (lay-out).

Outro aspecto importante é a hierarquia fortemente visível entre os quartos: dois dormitórios de dimensões e formas parecidas e uma suíte, reservada ao casal, composta por banheiro exclusivo, closet e sacada. A sala de estar/jantar coloca-se à frente dos demais ambientes e funciona como filtro entre o interior e o exterior.

CONSIDERAÇÕES FINAIS

O quadro abaixo indica as áreas de cada setor e em relação à área total dos respectivos apartamentos, e a diferença, em módulo, entre elas:

Setor	Percentual	Percentual	Diferença em Módulo	Diferença em Área (m2)
	Brasil	Alemanha		
Setor Social	32,20%	21,80%	10,40%	11,44
Setor Íntimo	41,80%	49,60%	7,80%	8,58
Setor de Serviços	22,00%	11,80%	10,20%	11,22
Circulação	4,00%	16,80%	12,80%	14,08
Total	100,00%	100,00%		

Tabela 03: Quadro de Áreas em Comparação

Percebe-se através deste quadro comparativo (tabela 03), que no exemplo brasileiro os setores sociais e de serviço são maiores que no caso alemão, assim como neste segundo são maiores os valores para o setor íntimo e para a circulação.

Examinando estes dados, chegamos às seguintes informações:

O setor social brasileiro é maior principalmente porque a sala de estar/jantar contém uma circulação que lhe é implícita; já na Alemanha a área da circulação é maior, mas ela está fisicamente separada e bem definida;

O setor íntimo alemão é maior porque os dormitórios têm áreas maiores, entretanto, no Brasil encontramos a suíte, a quantidade de banheiros é maior e o seu uso diferenciado, isto é, um social e outro íntimo;

O setor de serviços brasileiro também é maior em função da área de serviço e da dependência de empregada.

Voltando à proposição de que os modos e cultura do morar correspondem também às normas da sociedade, e às informações adquiridas através do estudo comparativo entre as plantas baixas dos apartamentos de Freiburg i.B. e de Florianópolis/SC, presume-se que a sociedade brasileira é mais hierarquizada e formal do que a alemã, resultado de uma estrutura familiar patriarcal tradicional e de origem latina.

Os resultados desta estrutura patriarcal são percebidos, por exemplo, na localização e acesso do setor íntimo, ficando normalmente o quarto do casal em posição mais reservada. Ainda por este motivo, o papel desempenhado pela mulher também se mostra elucidativo e visível nas diferenças entre as áreas dos setores de serviço, assim como nas escalas de transição entre as áreas públicas e privadas da moradia e do exterior.

Outro ponto que merece destaque é a crescente vinculação da moradia brasileira aos sistemas de condomínios, em conseqüência da violência e (causa) da falta de espaços públicos das cidades, que induzem aos encontros dentro do espaço privado da casa.

As diferenças apontadas nesta pesquisa podem ser facilmente verificadas no cotidiano das relações sociais e familiares de ambos os países: resultados de suas histórias e seus ideais de produção e reprodução sociais, isto é, das formas de legitimação de cada sociedade.

Notas:

1
HÄUβERMANN, Hartmut & SIEBEL, Walter. *Soziologie des Wohnens: eine Enführung in Wandel und Ausdiffrenzierung des Wohnens*. München: Juventa Verlag, 1996, p.44.

2
Id., Ibid., p.11.

3
Freiburg im Breisgau. *Stadt Freiburg*. Disponível em <http://www.freiburg.de> Acessado em 22/02/2005.

4
Id., Ibid.

5
ImmobilienScout24. Disponível em <www.scout24.de> Acessado em 05/06/2006.

6
O *Deutsches Institut für Normung* (seu nome comercial é DIN), com sede em Berlim, é o órgão nacional de normalização da Alemanha. Elabora, em cooperação com o comércio, a indústria, a ciência, os consumidores e instituições públicas, padrões técnicos (normas) para a racionalização e a garantia da qualidade. O DIN representa os interesses dos alemães nas organizações internacionais de normalização (ISO, CEI, etc.).

Referências Adicionais:

Baugesetzbuch. 38. Edição. München: Beck Text im Deutscher Tascehnbuch Verlag, 2005.

Deutsches Institut für Normung – DIN. Disponível em <http://www2.din.de/index.php?lang=en> Acessado em 19/06/2006.

Guia Floripa. *Informações turísticas e geográficas de Florianópolis.* Disponível em <http://www.guiafloripa.com.br/cidade/dadosgeo.php3> Acesso em 23/02/2005.

Hantei Engenharia. Disponível em <www.hantei.com.br> Acessado em 05/06/2006.

Presidência da República Federativa do Brasil. *Lei Federal n° 6766.* Disponível em <https://www.planalto.gov.br/ccivil_03/LEIS/L6766.htm> Acessado em 12/06/2006.

Verticalização e Edifícios de Apartamentos em João Pessoa: considerações preliminares

Preliminary analysis of vertical growth in João Pessoa, Brazil.

Carolina Chaves

When I taught a seminar on the Global Apartments issue at the Graduate Program in Architecture at the Federal University of Rio Grande do Norte (PPGAU-UFRN), Carolina Chaves was still an undergrad student at UFPB in João Pessoa but she wrote the best paper in my class. Despite being so young she was already working as a research assistant to Nelci Tinem, and performing like an experienced graduate. In this chapter, based on her graduation thesis, Chaves look at the roots of vertical growth in João Pessoa and what she uncovered applies to most Brazilian mid-size cities. Thirsty for development and an image of modernity, cities all over Brazil subsidized vertical growth when there was no real reason for it, privileging upper income segments with fiscal incentives for replicating in apartments the social structure (read segregation) of their comfortable homes.

"Debater o moderno na América Latina é debater a cidade: a cidade americana não é apenas o produto mais genuíno da modernidade ocidental, mas também, ademais, é um produto criado como uma máquina para inventar a modernidade, estendê-la e reproduzi-la".
(Adrián Gorelik)

Partidários da idéia expressa por Gorelik, e tentando compreender os processos que marcam a construção da modernidade urbana, buscamos identificar e discutir seus símbolos a partir da prática de arquitetura e do discurso que a legitima, tendo por estudo de caso a experiência moderna da cidade de João Pessoa, capital da Paraíba, no quadro da produção da Arquitetura Moderna Brasileira no que excede seus centros hegemônicos – Rio de Janeiro e São Paulo.

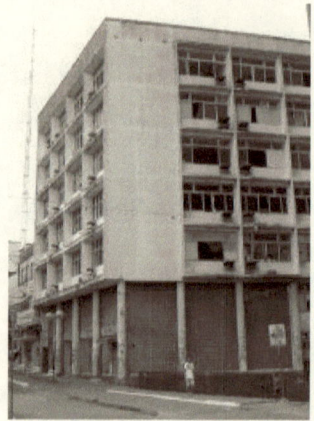

Figura 1: Prédio sede do IPASE. Fonte: arquivo pessoal da autora.

A produção de arquitetura moderna nesses centros urbanos outros é um processo que está, no Brasil, essencialmente ligado à pós-segunda Guerra Mundial, à saída de G. Vargas do cenário político e ao início do Estado desenvolvimentista, o que nos faz partir da segunda metade da década de 1940. João Pessoa mostra os primeiros traços dessa modernidade nos últimos anos da década de 1940 quando foi construído o prédio sede do IPASE[1] (Figura 1), inaugurado em 1951, e cujo impacto pode ser percebido na transcrição abaixo:

"Localizado no Ponto de Cem Réis, **o prédio do IPASE dá um toque de progresso à fisionomia da cidade alta, onde ainda dominam as antigas construções de aspécto provinciano**. Constitue [sic], com a graça das suas linhas, um marco de transformação urbana em área que mais tem resistido ao surto inovador da arquitetura moderna" [grifo nosso]. (POSTAL..., 1953, P.03).

---

[1] Instituto de Aposentadoria e Pensões dos Servidores do Estado.

Nessa obra, já podemos perceber algumas marcas dessa nova modernidade[2] expressa através de uma arquitetura moderna admirada pela "graça de suas linhas", uma modernidade positiva que viria atestar o progresso. Nesse momento, outro elemento expressivo é incorporado à paisagem da cidade: a verticalização. De fato, o prédio do IPASE, com seus 09 pavimentos, é o primeiro a romper com a horizontalidade do centro da cidade e a abrir uma perspectiva que só seria explorada uma década mais tarde com a construção do Edifício Presidente João Pessoa e que marca o início do primeiro ciclo de verticalização da cidade, e é concluído com a construção do edifício Manoel Pires. Em ambos aparece a unidade habitacional do apartamento.

No projeto de construção dessa cidade moderna, progressista e desenvolvimentista, se por um lado o arranha-céu surge com grande força simbólica, por outro é o programa habitação que corporifica as relações de formação dessa sociedade assimilando os desejos da nova modernidade. É, portanto, a habitação o principal vetor de difusão da linguagem de arquitetura moderna na cidade de João Pessoa. Teixeira (2008, p.83), estudando a difusão da arquitetura moderna nessa cidade afirma que:

"Com efeito, o setor habitacional tinha um peso significativo na transformação da paisagem urbana da cidade [de João Pessoa], não só do ponto de vista quantitativo como também qualitativo. A modernização da arquitetura era diretamente remetida às novas residências que então surgiam".

Lilian Vaz (2002, p.17) destaca, ainda, a habitação como o "mais importante elemento do ambiente construído", e assenta essa idéia dizendo que como "parte integrante do cotidiano, a habitação interfere nas práticas sociais, apóia a memória individual e coletiva, guardando significados para os diversos segmentos da população e participando da formação das identidades sociais. Encontra-se, portanto, no centro da relação espaço-sociedade".

---

[2] Falamos aqui em 'nova modernidade' por entender que esta resultada de uma nova lógica, de um novo quadro ideológico, diverso daquele que promoveu as primeiras ações de modernização das cidades brasileiras claramente de inspiração Haussmanniana.

O arranha-céu, marca visual do centro de negócios, é de fato um dos grandes símbolos dessa modernidade refletindo o progresso e o desenvolvimento da cidade. Nesse quadro, o novo programa habitacional (apartamentos) para classe média alta surge dentro de um discurso que procura legitimar o espírito dos novos tempos, do habitante da 'metrópole', ao mesmo tempo em que reflete um novo quadro social e novos valores culturais. Sem dúvida, esse processo não acontece sem resistências. Nos jornais são divulgadas algumas notas de 'protesto' ao que vai se transformando a paisagem da cidade, as quais são vistas em geral como expressão nostálgica de homens passadistas, que não sabem enxergar o progresso. Nessas bases é construído o discurso de construção da cidade moderna, cujas marcas de modernidade estão impressas, dentre outras formas, nos prédios altos e no desenho dos novos apartamentos.

"Isso constitui [a construção de um prédio de 12 andares no centro da cidade], motivo de satisfação para uma grande maioria. Mas há os saudosistas, almas provincianas que vêem essa transformação com um ranço de amargura". (CRESCER..., 1963, p.03).

Nesse momento, a produção de arquitetura está essencialmente atrelada à ação da iniciativa privada quando se especializa o mecanismo de construção nas ações de incorporadores, construtores e um novo quadro de arquitetos e engenheiros e de um mercado consumidor em formação, constantemente instigado a consumir – produtos e idéias.

"... desmontem-se os pardieiros [edificações térreas] e ergam-se prédios que enchem as vistas e acomodem lojas e mais lojas, gente e mais gente.
Mas, para que isto aconteça, teremos de contar com a visão – será que ainda existe isso – dos **homens de negócios, os filhos (...) mais bem afortunados e... progressistas. Procedendo de maneira positiva os donos de fortunas, estarão empregando capitais num empreendimento rentabilíssimo e demonstrando amor pela cidade"** [grifo nosso]. (UM PROBLEMA..., 1966, p.07)

Assim, é comercializada a idéia da verticalização, e o prédio de apartamentos torna-se, então, símbolo da classe média alta com constantes referências a grandes centros como Rio de Janeiro, São Paulo e Recife. Essas referências trazem consigo soluções técnicas, formais e arranjos espaciais numa tentativa [talvez] de transplantar modos de vida. No entanto, delineia-se nesse momento, um dos questionamentos que alimentam as análises desse trabalho que é tentar perceber, mesmo que ainda se constitua em uma análise preliminar, os possíveis embates entre modernidade e tradição na apropriação dessas idéias por uma sociedade fortemente filiada aos seus quintais e casas isoladas.

Por outro lado, embora se identifique o papel da iniciativa privada, ela nunca prescinde a ação Estatal, uma vez que é esta que detém os mecanismos de regulamentação de ocupação e construção da cidade, como a elaboração de Códigos Municipais e Leis que incentivavam em seu texto a produção de prédios mais altos na cidade, que se em suas primeiras ações não definia zonas para esse 'aumento de gabarito', em 1957 delimita, com a Lei Municipal n° 440, determina:

"Fica proibida a construção de prédios inferiores a três andares nas Avenidas Guedes Pereira, Barão do Triunfo, Praças 1817, Vidal de Negreiros em João Pessoa, ruas Duque de Caxias e Visconde Pelotas".

Essa medida passa a determinar a verticalização (indo além de incentivá-la e se dirigiu a uma região determinada (TEIXEIRA, 2008, p.98), o que a torna semelhante a outras leis adotadas no país. Em João Pessoa, a Lei Municipal de n° 299, aprovada em 20 de julho de 1956, que estabeleceu:

"Art. 1° - Fica concedida isenção do imposto predial por 5 (cinco) anos, aos imóveis a serem construídos no perímetro urbano da cidade, com mais de 3 (três) pavimentos, desde que seus proprietários iniciem a construção dos mesmos, no prazo de 2 (dois) anos, a partir da publicação da presente lei". (JOÃO PESSOA, 1956).

A produção dessas construções faz-se em duas áreas da cidade (Fig. 2), a área central e dois bairros da faixa litorânea (Tambaú e Cabo Branco). O primeiro representa o centro de

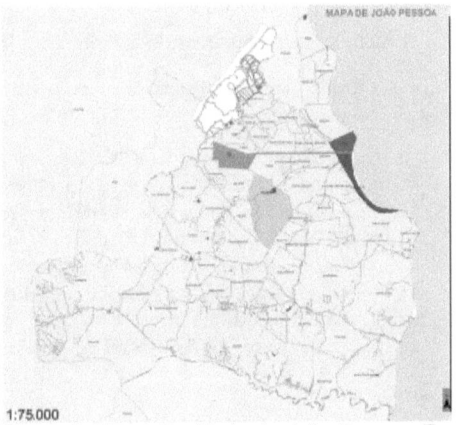

Figura 2: Mapa da cidade de João Pessoa. Em destaque as áreas de estudo: Centro, Tambaú e Cabo Branco . Fonte: PMJP, editado pela autora (2008).

negócios da cidade e uma área com infra-estrutura consolidada; o segundo, o novo setor de expansão da cidade claramente marcado pela ocupação da classe economicamente dominante. Nesse processo de ocupação os prédios de apartamento aparecem como figuras marcantes, especialmente na área litorânea onde o programa habitacional caracteriza essa produção – na área central, ele ainda divide espaço com prédios de serviço, comércio e institucionais.

Vê-se que dos vinte (20) projetos de edifícios altos construídos em João Pessoa entre os anos de 1958 e 1975, oito (08) apresentam programa residencial multifamiliar. Desse total, apenas dois (02) são mistos: Ed. Pres. João Pessoa (residencial/institucional) e Ed. Manoel Pires (residencial/comercial). Percebe-se ainda que a grande maioria dessas construções ocorre na década de 1960, particularmente marcada pelo ano de 1964 quando é criado o BNH (Banco Nacional da Habitação).

Essas ações estão vinculadas as campanhas midiáticas de incentivo à aquisição da casa própria, amparada no discurso de modernidade intrínseco ao processo de desenvolvimento da cidade, o qual é viabilizado economicamente por programas de financiamento para construção e aquisição da casa própria, o que fica evidente quando os jornais noticiam a ajuda do financiamento da Caixa Econômica Federal[3] para conclusão de obras interrompidas, exemplo do edifício Caricé, ou quando os encartes publicitários fazem referência direta a essas linhas de crédito para compra ou construção.

"A Caixa Econômica Federal da Paraíba assinará o maior contrato individual de financiamento através dos recursos do Banco Nacional de Habitação (Plano Impacto), para conclusão de conjuntos e edifícios residenciais cujas obras, após terem sido adiantadas em 75 por cento do total, hajam sido paralizadas [sic] por falta de recursos.
... o financiamento será da ordem de noventa milhões de cruzeiros velhos, **destinando-se à conclusão do Edifício Caricé**, um dos maiores do Norte [entenda-se Nordeste], em área coberta, atualmente em construção nessa Capital e que contará com cêrca [sic] de 135 apartamentos" [grifo nosso]. (CAIXA..., 1967, p.01)

---

[3] Banco vinculado ao BNH (Banco Nacional da Habitação).

O primeiro desses prédios construído (Fig. 3), o Ed. Presidente João Pessoa (1957) – apesar de ainda anterior às ações do BNH[4] – surgiu dentro do programa de incentivo a casa própria promovido pelo IAPB (Instituto de Aposentadoria e Pensões dos Bancários) – integrante do programa nacional dos IAPs (Instituto de Aposentadoria e Pensões), composto por outros cinco institutos. Dentre esses institutos, o IAPB era o que apresentava melhor padrão de construção, por gerir

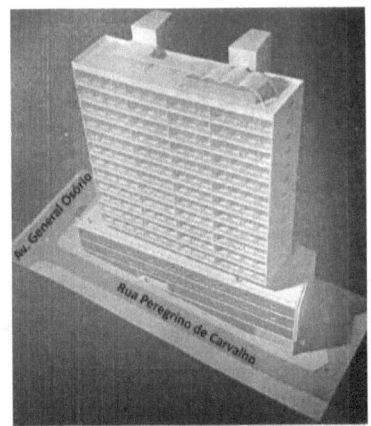

Figura 3: Maquete Ed. Presidente João Pessoa (1957). Fonte: Revista dos Bancários (1958), editado pela autora (2008).

recursos maiores. Isso fica evidente na construção do ed. Pres. João Pessoa, popularmente conhecido por "18 andares", numa referência explícita ao número de seus pavimentos, o que até mesmo para a produção dos institutos é uma exceção num conjunto de edificações de alturas médias (entre 05 e 10 pavimentos), o que dispensava, em regra, o uso do elevador (item caro à construção).

Da mesma forma que o projeto para o prédio do IPASE, o projeto do Ed. 18 Andares também marca a adoção de um programa construtivo que não era habitual à tradição local – seja por suas características plásticas e formais seja por suas soluções técnicas (é evidente a racionalização da estrutura) e funcionais (ventilação, iluminação e circulação), bem como pelo desenho das unidades habitacionais, um esquema que se tornaria comum nas construções subseqüentes.

Assim, o arquiteto carioca Ulysses Burlamaqui elabora o projeto para o prédio sede do IAPB em João Pessoa, e que anexava em seu programa o plano da

---

[4] Em verdade, o BNH é criado em substituição aos IAPs dentro de uma ação federal que objetivada ampliar o acesso à moradia às populações de baixa renda, lembrando que as ações do segundo também atendam ao princípio da habitação social.

moradia multi-familiar para seus associados. A implantação de um exemplar da arquitetura moderna brasileira – made in Rio de Janeiro para a capital paraibana –, abre caminhos para se pensar a extensão desse movimento.

A construção da obra é marcada por muita expectativa, sendo constantes as notícias nos jornais anunciando seu início para o ano de 1958, ano seguinte à aprovação. No entanto, a relutância dos pensionistas em morar em um prédio tão alto e implantado em terreno inclinado fez que com muitas famílias só aceitassem mudar-se para os novos apartamentos alguns anos depois. Era o ineditismo da construção, a estranheza da implantação e a pouca afeição a esses novos hábitos de morar em apartamentos, um tal morar moderno.

Pela própria natureza do programa, o apartamento exige maior aproveitamento de área condensando os espaços em tamanho e em proximidade. Com efeito, a setorização dos espaços por suas funções fica clara no desenho do apartamento, mas os cômodos agora encontram-se desconcertantemente próximos para a família tradicional burguesa, onde a transição entre social-íntimo-serviço se reduz a uma pequena circulação e finas paredes (Fig. 4).

A compreensão das semelhanças entre os desenhos das plantas de apartamento, vistos em diferentes projetos produzidos em tantas outras localidades, reside por um lado na pertença a um movimento que toma proporções internacionais e, por outro, na gênese própria desse tipo de construção que surge das experiências européias da década de 1920 na busca por um módulo habitacional mínimo – economicamente viável – e que, naquele contexto, vinculava-se essencialmente à habitação social.

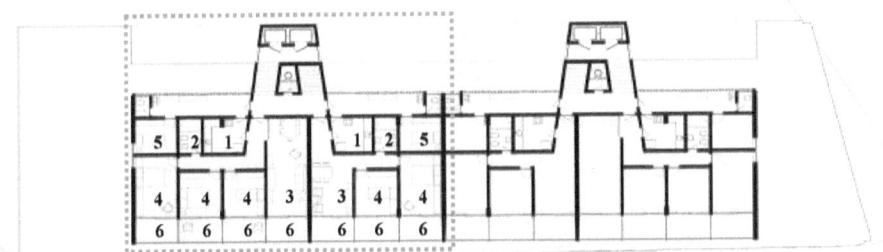

Figura 5: Ed. Presidente João Pessoa ("18 andares"). Planta baixa pavimento tipo. Apartamentos com 03 e 02 dormitórios. Fonte: acervo 18 andares, digitalizado por Carolina Chaves e Olívia Poliana (2005), editado pela autora. (1) cozinha, (2) Banheiro, (3) Sala, (4) dormitórios, (5) dependência de empregada e (6) varanda.

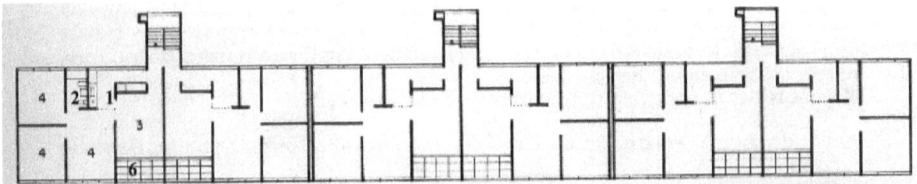

Figura 5: Conjunto Residencial Vila Giomar, em Santo André, arquiteto Carlos F. Ferreira, 1949 (IAPI). Planta do pavimento tipo: circulação vertical independente (MINDLIN, 2000). (1) cozinha, (2) banheiro, (3) sala, (4) dormitórios e (5) varanda.

No Brasil, é interessante perceber que o programa habitacional multi-familiar se desenvolve sob duas bases com perfis bem distintos: a da habitação social, e da produção imobiliária para classe média alta. E mais curioso ainda, é que, no processo de apropriação dessa linguagem, enquanto essas iniciativas fracassam no primeiro grupo, legitima-se a idéia do prédio de apartamentos como símbolo de desenvolvimento e poder da classe dominante. Assim, a apropriação desses espaços por esta classe aponta a introdução de um espaço particular no desenho da habitação: a dependência de empregada. Vindo de uma sociedade escravocrata, os serviços da casa ainda fazem parte dos encargos de empregados domésticos – em João Pessoa, a retirada desses espaços, se atualmente já se tornou comum em centros como São Paulo ou Rio de Janeiro, não se faz sem resistências nas recentes incorporações.

A observação dos desenhos anteriores (Fig. 4 e 5) também demonstra a diferença de padrão da construção desse instituto [IAPB] à medida que o edifício dos bancários amplia a varanda (dimensão 'pública' das unidades 'privadas') e o uso de elevadores (04 unidades). Nesse sentido, são associadas soluções vistas em prédios de apartamentos de outros centros urbanos

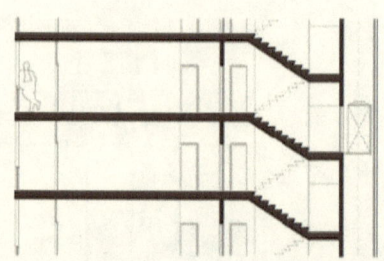

Fig. 6: Detalhe do corte transversal mostrando o esquema da circulação proposta. Desenho: Carolina Chaves e Olívia Polyana, editado pela autora.

– ex., Ed. Louveira, em São Paulo – destinados à classe média alta, como a tentativa de reduzir áreas de circulação horizontal e otimizar o uso dos elevadores com paradas intermediárias entre pisos (Fig. 6).

Ainda durante a construção do Ed. Pres. João Pessoa, formula-se a tentativa de construção de outro edifício de apartamentos [agora exclusivamente para este fim], que seria construído também na área central. O projeto de autoria de Florismundo Lins e Heleny Lins – ele, arquiteto radicado no Recife e formado pela Faculdade Nacional de Arquitetura (RJ), portanto conhecer da produção dos grandes centros –, publicado em 1959 pela revista Acrópole (Fig. 7 e 8), traz no desenho de suas unidades habitacionais arranjos espaciais curiosos [até certo ponto inovadores para o que era comum para esse tipo de programa habitacional].

Os fatos que envolvem a elaboração e construção do ed. Caricé expõe o claro embate entre arquitetura e mercado imobiliário em um prenúncio, por um lado, do declínio da hegemonia do projeto

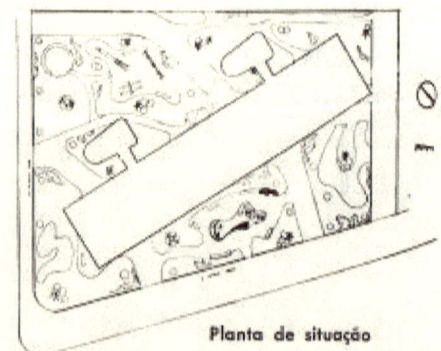

Planta de situação

Fig. 7: Ed. Caricé. Projeto de 1959 elaborado pelos arquitetos Florismundo e Heleny Lins. Fonte: Revista Acrópole, editado pela autora (2008).

de arquitetura moderna – da aceitação de seus princípios característicos – e, por outro lado, dos meios de apropriação pelo incorporador imobiliário dos traços formais que dariam a sua obra o status de uma obra "moderna", que se converte em forte argumento publicitário. Embora o projeto não tenha sido levado a diante, por alegar seu incorporador "mau aproveitamento do terreno", a análise de seus espaços habitacionais é válida enquanto concepção projetual.

Os arquitetos pernambucanos propõem uma edificação com 10 pavimentos apoiados sobre uma galeria de pilotis, que abrigaria ainda um mezanino, e cuja implantação seria completamente solta do lote aproveitando a área livre com um paisagismo de formas livres. Nesse projeto o 'pilotis' assume seu genuíno papel de liberar o solo urbano para o passeio público[5].

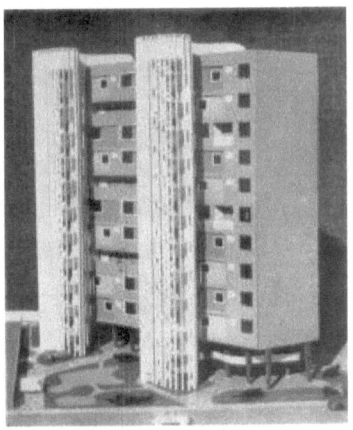

A composição formal traz referências do projeto de Lúcio Costa para o parque Guinle (1948) nos volumes de circulação vertical e da composição das fachadas faz lembrar o Ed. Esther (1934-36), de Vital Brazil e Ademar Marinho, cuja complexidade do programa e variação dos tipos de apartamentos propostos também resulta na combinação de diversos elementos plásticos.

Figura 8: Edifício Caricé, maquete do projeto de 1959, fachada norte. Destaque para o tratamento das colunas de circulação vertical e paisagismo. Fonte: Revista Acrópole (1959), editado pela autora (2008).

O desenho desses apartamentos traz ricas informações sobre a concepção desses novos espaços [apartamentos], a exemplo da maneira como o quarto de empregada se apresenta nas diferentes propostas de planta. Ora mudando de posição, ora de tamanho, mas sempre presente, esse cômodo sempre agregado ao setor dos serviços, volta-se para dentro das habitações de tamanho médio, tornando-se maior nos apartamentos

---

[5] O que se observa nos outros projetos, inclusive na proposta final para o Ed. Caricé, é o uso do pilotis para liberação do solo para uso privado de estacionamento do prédio.

maiores (comportando até três empregados) – o que logo se relaciona ao status da família – ou, abrindo para circulação externa à unidade habitacional nos apartamentos menores. Nos apartamentos maiores a setorização é mais marcante e surgem novos espaços: gabinete, bar, separação das salas de estar e jantar, sala de música e a suíte (dormitório com banheiro privado[6]. Essa separação das salas reflete, de algum modo, o uso das áreas sociais da casa burguesa. Esse arranjo abre caminho para se questionar até onde persistem os traços da casa tradicional na proposta da unidade de habitação moderna.

Os incorporadores, eng. Romildo Marques de Almeida, e Walter Vinagre, propuseram outro projeto (Fig. 9 e 10) para o local, executado entre os anos de 1964 e 1968. O novo projeto corresponde a uma planta em "L", que define o pavimento tipo com cinco apartamentos e que será repetido ao longo de 13 pavimentos, ampliando o número de apartamentos para 65. Duas outras alterações são destacadas, uma de ordem espacial, que se refere ao fechamento da área frontal do lote com muros que reservam o espaço térreo, liberado pelos pilotis, para o uso de estacionamento pelos moradores, que propõe o uso de apenas um volume para circulação vertical, no lugar dos dois propostos anteriormente. No novo arranjo proposto, os apartamentos retomam o arranjo espacial já comentado e que será recorrente nos projetos desse período.

O novo empreendido é divulgado em Campina Grande[7], cidade do brejo paraibano e potencial público consumidor, em um exemplo da forte associação da verticalidade ao progresso e à modernidade:

---

[6] Composição pouco comum e que só se concretizou, nesse período, no edifício de apartamentos João Marques de Almeida [em uma das suas 05 unidades, o que pode apontar para uma experimentação] e, voltará a aparecer apenas na década de 1970, no edifício de apartamentos Manoel Pires, agora como proposta consciente, integrada a todas as unidades habitacionais.

[7] Campina Grande, a cidade que mais cresce no interior do Estado, sempre disputou com João Pessoa, a capital, em desenvolvimento urbano, econômico, demográfico e, até mesmo, a condição de capital do Estado. Dessa forma, sempre foi constante o afluxo de visitantes vindos de Campina para temporadas na capital ora pelos negócios, ora para o veraneio.

"O início das obras do Edifício CARICÉ marca o começo [sic] de uma nova era de progresso para a capital paraibana, no campo imobiliário. (...) Veja, também, em pleno funcionamento o numeroso número de máquinas". (EDIFÍCIO Caricé, 1964, p.5).

Em 1962 é aprovado o projeto do edifício Borborema a ser construído no bairro do Cabo Branco (Fig. 2) com 13 pavimentos, e cuja construção só se

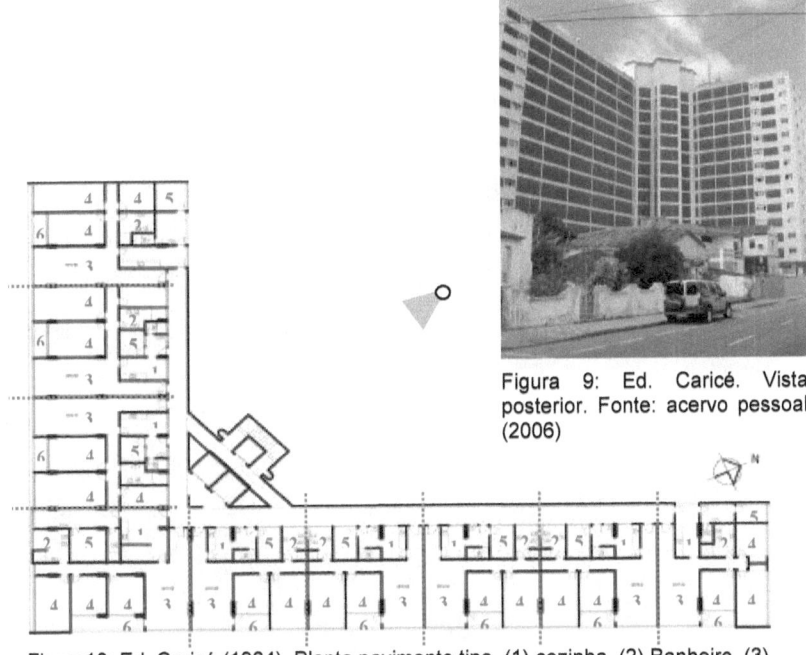

Figura 9: Ed. Caricé. Vista posterior. Fonte: acervo pessoal (2006)

Figura10: Ed. Caricé (1964). Planta pavimento tipo. (1) cozinha, (2) Banheiro, (3) Sala, (4) dormitórios, (5) dependência de empregada, (6) varanda. Desenho: Camilla Duarte et al.. editado pela autora.

iniciaria dois anos mais tarde, o que coincide com o ano de 1964 e os incentivos às construções residenciais. Após a experiência do "18 Andares", os projetos executados na cidade de João Pessoa são elaborados por profissionais inseridos no mercado imobiliário local e, em sua grande maioria, com formação acadêmica na Escola de Belas Artes do Recife[8], que contribuem para consolidar a produção local de arquitetura moderna.

Embora se fale agora em produção local, é fácil constatar as aproximações do programa local aos programas de edifícios altos construídos em outros centros urbanos e torna-se recorrente o grande volume prismático de seção retangular, que abriga as unidades habitacionais dispostas de forma contígua, evidenciando o sistema estrutural adotado, e o volume que corresponde à circulação vertical. Nesse sentido, são evidentes as semelhanças entre os edifícios Pres. João Pessoa e Borborema, seja na escolha formal, seja no desenho das habitações (Fig. 12) [o que pode ser percebido nos projetos comentados na seqüência]. Permanece, então, a setorização social-íntimo-serviço e a pequena circulação linear mediando esses espaços, assim como o uso das paradas intermediárias para o elevador social[9].

Em 1965 foi aprovado o projeto do Ed. João Marques de Almeida, construído sob incorporação da IMPALA Imobiliária Paraibana Ltda e projeto assinado pelo eng. Romildo Marques de Almeida. As obras são iniciadas em dezembro de 1965 e ratificam a condição de símbolo de modernidade expressa na figura do arranha-céu.

"Com suas linhas modernas, o edifício João Marques de Almeida será, sem dúvida, uma das grandes contribuições que a iniciativa privada de João Pessoa vem dando embelezamento do aspécto [sic] urbanístico da nossa praia mais famosa". (PEDRA..., 1965, p.08).

Edifício residencial com doze (12) pavimentos, o João Marques de Almeida, que conta com 05 apartamentos por andar, num total de 60 unidades

---

[8] Até 1974 – ano da abertura do curso de Arquitetura e Urbanismo – os arquitetos que atuam em João Pessoa são, em sua grande maioria, graduados pela Escola de Belas Artes de Recife (Estado visinho), e alguns poucos do Rio de Janeiro.

[9] O elevador de serviço funciona normalmente, parando em seus respectivos pavimentos, e encontra-se no interior do volume residencial, enquanto o outro se destaca na volumetria como elemento compositivo.

habitacionais, traz uma proposta de ocupação diferente dos projetos anteriores, dividindo o lote em duas grandes áreas livres.

As unidades habitacionais (Fig. 13) que compõem o pavimento tipo são de 05 tipos diferente: A, B, C, D e E. As unidades D e E são os únicos exemplos, construídos, de habitação sem quarto de empregada – embora haja o banheiro de serviço – e suíte, respectivamente. As demais unidades, embora sigam arranjo espacial já mencionado, a separação entre área íntima e social-serviço é reforçada pela porta que individualiza essas áreas, ficando a pequena circulação entre os cômodos também de uso íntimo.

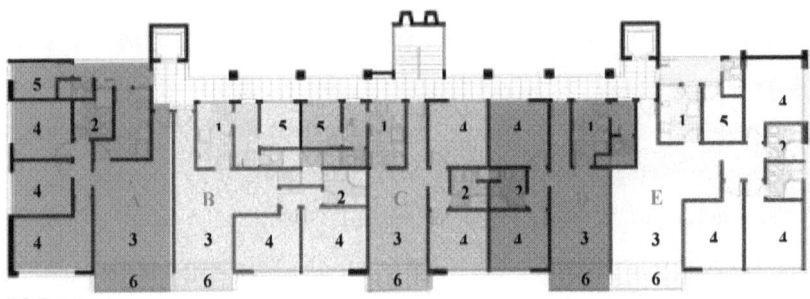

Figura 6: Ed. João Marques de Almeida, 1965. Planta baixada Pavimento Tipo. Fonte: PMJP, digitalizado pela autora (2008). (1) cozinha, (2) banheiro, (3) sala, (4) dormitórios, (5) dependência de empregada, (6) varanda. Fonte: PMJP, editado pela autora (2009).

Os projetos aprovados em 1968 marcam a continuação da escolha da orla para construção de edifícios altos residenciais, a exemplo dos Ed. Beiramar e São Marcos, os últimos a serem construídos na praia nesse primeiro ciclo de verticalização da cidade[10]. O primeiro, projetado pelo próprio incorporador, eng. Local Walter Vinagre, compõe a volumetria a partir da junção de dois blocos residenciais articulados pela coluna de circulação vertical, resultando em

---

[10] O próximo momento de verticalização da cidade ocorre a partir da década de 1980 e se caracteriza como um processo especulativo e de reprodução do solo urbana, e não mais como parte de um processo de construção da imagem de cidade moderna, que caracteriza esse primeiro momento. No caso específico da orla, no final dos anos de 1970 iniciam discussões sobre os gabaritos de suas futuras construções, quando é estabelecido o escalonamento de alturas. Assim, a altura à beira-mar fica limitada a até três (03) pavimentos.

uma planta em forma de 'H'. Os blocos são exatamente iguais e os apartamentos pouco variam entre si. Com efeito, o desenho das habitações modifica muito pouco o já comentado, salvo a inversão do quarto de empregada com a cozinha, agora um pouco afastada da sala. Assim, a cozinha 'invade' o setor íntimo da casa dividindo a mesma circulação de acesso aos quartos e ao banheiro social. O segundo, projetado pelo arquiteto Mário Di Lascio e incorporado pela empresa local Predial Cabo Branco, distancia-se um pouco do bloco prismático retangular que abriga o conjunto de apartamento do edifício. O arquiteto projeta duas torres, cada uma com dois apartamentos, articulados também pela coluna de circulação vertical.

Nesse arranjo a separação entre setor íntimo e de serviços é completa, onde as salas [conformando um "L" em planta] compõem o espaço de transição entre os mesmos. O setor íntimo é preservado até mesmo do acesso social, em algo semelhante às unidades habitacionais do Ed. João Marques de Almeida.

Aprovado em 1975, o Ed. Manoel Pires (arq. Carneiro da Cunha), construído no centro de negócios da capital, traz o programa habitacional associado ao uso comercial no bloco inferior, fruto da iniciativa do comerciante Manoel Pires. No quadro dos projetos já analisados, esse projeto destaca-se por surgir dois (02) anos após a elaboração do Código de Obras da Cidade, o que pode apontar os caminhos para perceber algumas modificações no desenho do apartamento, como a proposição da suite, agora como indicação legislativa.

Os apartamentos sobrepõem-se como casas isoladas umas sobre as outras, o que desvirtua, em parte, a idéia de habitação multifamilar a partir de unidades geminadas. Se esse recurso individualiza esse projeto dos anteriormente expostos, o arranjo espacial dessas "casas de apartamento" retoma a setorização presente na maioria dos projetos anteriores: setor social ligado ao setor de serviços e ao setor íntimo, enquanto estes dois últimos são dissociados, e uma pequena circulação comum e de transição entre setores.

Decerto, a introdução do novo programa multi-familiar não ocorreu sem despertar oposições, particularmente uma rejeição que tentava se sustentar na tradição, na manutenção de antigos hábitos vinculados à casa isolada, ao quintal e à cidade que cresce horizontalmente, espraiando-se e não adensando. Trata-se, portanto, do embate entre modernização e cultura local [um dos focos da pesquisa que dá continuidade às análises preliminares sobre habitação e arquitetura moderna em João Pessoa]. No entanto, a continuidade do processo de construção desses edifícios demonstra o forte apelo às imagens de progresso e desenvolvimento vinculadas ao projeto de construção de uma cidade moderna, que ao mesmo tempo assinala mudanças na maneira de como habitá-la.

Aquilo que nós nordestinos possuímos diferentes dos grandes centros sulistas, a vida em residências térreas, ajardinadas e muradas, além do quintal onde se plantava o tradicional mamão e outras fruteiras, está sendo invadida modificada pelos prédios de apartamentos que se levantam destruindo a estática [sic] de uma cidade natural pela sua arquitetura e espaço, imprópria a semelhantes sistemas de moradias.

"Não temos necessidade de gaiolas de arranha-céus. O município João Pessoa, por exemplo, caberá dez, vinte vezes folgada, a população atual, com suas casas isoladas, de jardins e quintais. Esses absurdos que contaminam a paisagem urbanística [sic] se são impróprios à atividade pública, são nocivos à vida doméstica. Nossos prédios não deveriam ir além dos quatro pavimentos". (CRESCIMENTO ..., 1969, p.3)

Nesse trecho, não apenas o embate entre tradição e modernidade fica evidente, mas o caráter simbólico do primeiro ciclo de verticalização pelo qual passa a cidade de João Pessoa, uma vez que não estava em jogo a necessidade de adensamento, o que é explícito na ocupação dos bairros litorâneos (Tambaú, Cabo Branco, Manaíra) onde grande parte de seus terrenos encontravam-se vazios. Dessa forma, o edifício de apartamento, bem como o programa que o caracteriza, é introduzido na capital paraibana como parte de um processo que exógeno e legitimado pela idéia de progresso e desenvolvimento vinculados na mídia. Por fim, uma "questão de status" (EDIFÍCIO Manoel..., 1975, p.51).

De fato, as considerações aqui expostas sobre a verticalização e a produção de habitação multi-familiar (edifícios de apartamentos) para classe média alta na cidade de João Pessoa não são nada mais que preliminares e fruto de uma pesquisa em desenvolvimento junto ao programa de Pós-Graduação da Escola de Engenharia de São Carlos – USP. Ficam abertos, portanto, alguns caminhos para investigação e aprofundamento como em que termos se materializa o embate entre modernidade e tradição no programa das casas modernas contemporâneas aos primeiros edifícios de apartamentos ou através de uma análise comparativa entre o arranjo espacial das casas e dos apartamentos, como se processa a passagem do primeiro para o segundo?

Referencias:

CAIXA assinará contrato de financiamento. **Jornal A União**, João Pessoa, 17 mai. 67, p.1.

CHAVES, Carolina. **João Pessoa: verticalização, progresso e modernidade. Registro dos Prédios Altos 1958 – 1975**. João Pessoa: Trabalho Final de Graduação, UFPB, 2008.

_____. **Edf. Residencial Pres. João Pessoa e Edf. Caricé: João Pessoa e o Desafio das Habitações Multifamiliares**. Recife, I Docomomo N-NE, 2006.

CRESCER para cima. **Jornal A União**. João Pessoa, 05 mar. 1963, p.3.

CRESCIMENTO vertical. **Jornal A União**, João Pessoa, 23 fev. 1969, p.3.

EDIFÍCIO de apartamentos. **Acrópole**, São Paulo, n. 243, p.110-110, jan. 1959.

EDIFÍCIO João Marques de Almeida. **Jornal A União**, João Pessoa, 28 dez. 1965, p.8.

EDIFÍCIO Manoel Pires – questão de status – na área mais verde da cidade. **Paraíba, Ontem e Hoje**, João Pessoa, n. 1, p.51, 1975.

EDIFÍCIO Santa Rita. **Jornal O Norte**, João Pessoa, 26 nov. 1968, p.4.

GORELIK, Adrián (org.). **Narrativas da Modernidade**. Belo Horizonte: Editora UFMG. 2005.

JOÃO PESSOA. Lei no 299, de 20 de julho de 1956. Concede isenção de impostos e dá outras providências. **Câmara Municipal de João Pessoa**, João Pessoa.

LARA, Fernando Luiz. **Popular Modernism: an analysis of the acceptance of modern architecture in 1950s Brasil**. 2001. Tese (Doutorado) – University of Michigan, Michigan, 2001.

MINDLIN, Henrique. **Modern Architecture in Brazil**. Rio de Janeiro: Editora Aeroplano, 2000.

NA MAIS linda praia do nordeste..., **Jornal O Norte**, João Pessoa, João Pessoa, 3 jan. 1968, p.8.

NERY, Juliana Cardoso. **Configurações da Metrópole Moderna: Os Arranha-Céus de Belo Horizonte 1940/1960**. Salvador, 2002, 273p. Área de Concentração: Urbanismo. Orientador: Prof. Marco Aurélio A. de Filgueiras Gomes.

POSTAL da Província. Jornal A União, João Pessoa, 06 nov. 1953, p.3.

SOMEKH, Nadia. **A Cidade Vertical e o Urbanismo Modernizador (1920-1939)**. São Paulo: Studio Nobel: Editora da Universidade de São Paulo: FAPESP, 1997.

TEIXEIRA, Fúlvio. **Difusão da Arquitetura Moderna na Cidade de João Pessoa (1956-1974)**. São Paulo: Dissertação de Mestrado em Arquitetura e Urbanismo/USP, 2008.

UM PROBLEMA. **Jornal A União**. João Pessoa, 16 out. 1966, p.7.

VAZ. Lilian Fessler. Modernidade e Moradia: habitação coletiva no Rio de Janeiro século XIX e XX. Rio de Janeiro: 7Letras, 2002.

Changes in Korean Apartment Unit Plans (1990s to 2000s)

Transformações nas plantas de apartamentos sul-coreanos, 1990-2000.

Youngchul Kim + Fernando Lara

De todos os países que o Global Apartment Research Group estudou o caso sul-coreano foi o mais impressionante. Em primeiro lugar pela velocidade das transformações na Coréia do Sul. Arrasada pela guerra e absolutamente empobrecida em meados dos anos 50, a Coréia do Sul empreendeu um ambicioso programa de modernização que a transformou em um dos países mais ricos do mundo 50 anos depois. Neste tempo a construção civil foi uma das colunas mestras tanto da aceleração econômica quanto da criação de uma nova sociedade: capitalista, consumista e obcecada com educação e tecnologia. O fato de que hoje em dia na Coréia existe mais de 1 unidade habitacional para cada família é reflexo desta política e é muito interessante perceber que o valor da unidade se mantém em alta mesmo quando o déficit é teoricamente sanado. Os apartamentos de Seoul figuram entre os mais diversos de todo o nosso banco de dados principalmente pela forma agressiva com que buscam a orientação sul (na Coréia, mais do que aquecimento passivo e melhor luminosidade a abertura para o sul é sinal de boa fortuna) e a organização tri-partida da unidade com quartos em ambos os lados das salas. Apesar disso, os apartamentos de Seoul relevelaram-se mais integrados (e consequentemente menos privativos) que seus pares no Brasil ou na Índia.

This study investigates whether spatial analysis of Korean apartment plans can explain certain changes in the apartment unit design in relation to socio-cultural trends. Since apartments are the dominant housing type in Korea, these units need to include and to follow commonly shared characteristics of residents' preferences. This study seeks to analyze Korean apartments in order to clarify characteristics of Korean apartment housing. From this analysis, it will be revealed how spatial configuration is correlated to social implications in the Korean apartment.

In this study, the hypothesis being tested is whether apartment housing can be a reflection of common social values when these houses are being built. An apartment, which is a type of multi-family housing, is one of the major housing types in the world (Angel, 2000).

WHY APARTMENT?

Why does this research choose apartment housing to analyze spatial configuration and social implications? First of all, in Korea, about 53% of the population lived in apartment housings in 2005, while detached housing was about 33%[1]. According to Korean Statistical Information Service (2007), about 400 thousand apartment units have been built every year in Korea, which is 3.5% of existing housing stock. Furthermore, Korean apartment housing has become a popular housing type for from upper middle to working class since 1962 (Kang et al., 1999). Although the construction of apartments started in 1962, the proportion of apartments has dramatically increased more than that of other housing types. The percentage of apartment housing in residential building has moved from 1% in 1975

---

[1] Korean Statistical Information Service, 2007

to 53% in 2005. This affects the increase of the ratio of housing unit per household, and the ratio becomes more than 100% in 2005.

Moreover, the pre-sale process of apartment housing enhances real estate strategy and design approach to follow the preferences of people. The pre-sale process of building apartments follow these phases: 1) planning and designing apartments 2) marketing and selling apartments to those who want to buy 3) constructing apartments, and 4) living in and evaluating an apartment. The period from planning to selling an apartment is shorter than the period from constructing to evaluating apartment housing. However, in the situation of selling constructed housing, feedback from residents could take a couple years. The feedback in the pre-sale process can affect planning and designing apartment housing before the construction period, which is a relatively shorter period. According to the short-term feedback, a developer and/or a designer can modify an apartment plan to make it more popular and attract consumers. Thus, socio-cultural aspects of housing can be well integrated to apartment housing in Korea. Korean apartment housing can have a close relationship between spatial configuration and social demands of housing.

WHY SPACE SYNTAX?

Why does this study choose the space syntax as a tool? Hillier and Hanson explain socio-cultural order in the built environment by defining and using the spatial configuration (Hillier & Hanson, 1984). Hanson explains that the spatial configuration in the domestic space is related to design of house and socio-cultural order (Hanson, 1998). In addition, Hillier develops the meaning of configuration from 'pattern aspect' relationship to quantitative analysis in the built environment (Hillier, 1996).

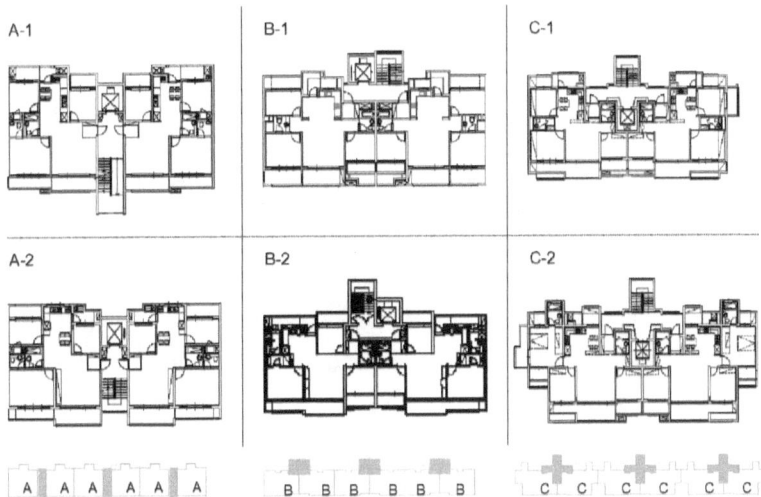

Figure 1 Selections of Korean Apartment Plans

Studies using the space syntax analysis have explained socio-cultural characteristics in domestic spaces. Monteiro (1997) explans social and cultural common elements of domestic spaces in Brazil by analyzing the integration values and the activity in different types and classes of domestic spaces. In addition, syntactical analysis of modern designed houses in Recife, Brazil is categorized as a typology of the social demands in Recife (Amorim, 1997). Amorim (2001) also finds that spatial indexes such as "the degree of permeability and relative connectivity" of houses based on the space syntax analysis is representative of the characteristics of domestic space in Brazil (see Amorim and Loureiro's chapter in this book). In our own research (Lara and Kim, JAPR, forthcoming), we used the space syntax to compare apartments in Brazil and Korea with promising results. Thus, the space syntax can be an appropriate theory and method in order to analyze spatial configuration and social implication in the Korean apartment housing.

METHODOLOGY

Six typical apartment unit plans from the late 1990s to the early 2000s are chosen for analyzing spatial configuration and socio-cultural elements in the apartment housing unit (Figure 1). These apartment units are all similar sized and intended for middle class families. They have three bedrooms, one living space, and one dining-kitchen space (3LDK) with two units sharing one staircase. These samples are categorized with three types (A, B, and C) according to those core styles, and each type has two sample unit plans.

Justified labeled graphs (J-graph) and integration values of each space in these units are drawn and analyzed. For the analysis of J-graph and visual integration in each unit, the Depthmap5.12r and the S3CONVEX2.0 are selected as computer applications2. This study has statistical limitations in generalizing the result because of the limited data. However, empirically representative data of the units can provide a basic analysis of each unit for future research.

PILOT STUDY

Before the analysis of the six sample plans, some Korean apartment housing units such as 3LDKs and 4LDKs are analyzed with the Depthmap in order to verify the relationship between the visual integration by the Depthmap and the previous studies of Korean apartment housing units. In Figure 2, the result of visual integration of apartment units by the Depthmap follows the conclusions of previous studies about the Korean apartment housing. Living and dining-kitchen spaces have high integration – red areas – in units, and the

---

[2] The Depthmap created by University College of London, and the S3CONVEX2.0 created by Seoul National University

biggest room of each unit is more integrative than the other rooms. The 3LDK have a similar spatial configuration as 4LDK (Choi, 1999; Kang et al., 1999; Choi, Cho, Park, & Park, 2004). In the unit plans of apartments, the living area and the dining-kitchen area is the center space semantically and syntactically, which is transformed from the courtyard of the traditional Korean urban house (Choi, 1999; Kang et al., 1999).

However, there are few previous studies of floor plans in apartment housing. The previous research about unit plans usually explains the characteristics of each space and analyzes these spatial configurations in these apartment units. These studies have focused on the domestic meaning rather than the design approach to develop and improve an apartment building. In addition, according to these visual integration maps of each unit, in a unit with windows of two opposite sides, one side has more importance because of its specific location.

Both sides of a unit have a balcony and windows. However, the living space is more integrated than the dining-kitchen space, and the balcony by the living space is also more integrated than the balcony by the dining-kitchen space.

3LDK

4LDK

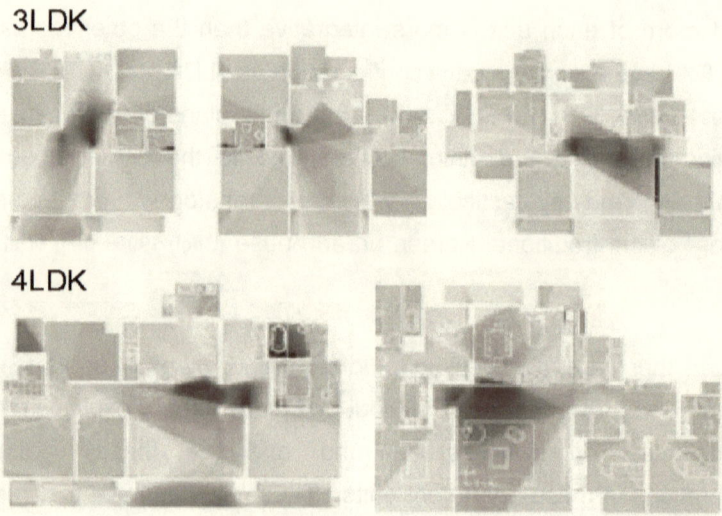

Figure 2 Pilot study of Unit Plans of Korean Apartment Housing

Therefore, this study analyzes floor plans as well as unit plans and seeks to interpret spatial orders and configuration in relation to social aspects in the Korean apartment housing. These apartment plans are analyzed in terms of two categories: unit plan and floor plan

RESULTS

Each 3LDK unit has three bedrooms, one living space, one dining & kitchen space, and two bathrooms. The area in each space is about 84m2. One of the differences among these unit plans is the width of units. While type A has two bay widths, type B and C has three bay widths. In addition, type C-2 has three and half bay widths. One of the bedrooms in type C-2 has two balconies of two opposite sides. Thus, if the living space is oriented to the south, all of bedrooms in the unit type C-2 can have southern daylight.

In addition, positions of doors to hall spaces are different among type A, B, and C. These doors at the entrance are related to the privacy of the domestic space side by side (Figure 3). The doors of type A face each other. In the types B and C, the entrance doors are oriented to the same side. Thus, while the floor plan of type A has weak protection of the privacy in each unit, the layout of type B and C can keep the inside of each unit from being exposed to people who live in the other unit.

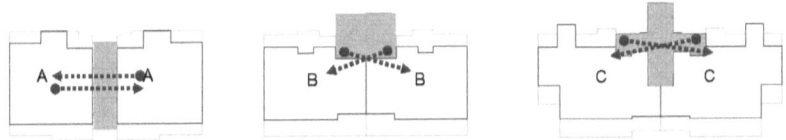

Figure 3 Privacy problems between two units in the different types of floor plan (Type A, Type B, and Type C)

First, according to the convex map of each unit (Figure 4), living space has the highest integration value in each unit. This result follows the previous research that living space is the central space in apartment units (강부성 Kang et al., 1999). Even though the unit design with living space, dining-kitchen, bedrooms, bathrooms, balconies, and entrance are different among these types, living space is the center in the spatial configuration of each unit.

In addition, the dining-kitchen space has the second highest integration value (Table 1). Integration values of the dining & kitchen spaces are greater than one except in type B-1 (Table 1). These dining-kitchen spaces are also a highly integrated space in the unit similar to the living spaces. Thus, these two spaces – living space and dining-kitchen space

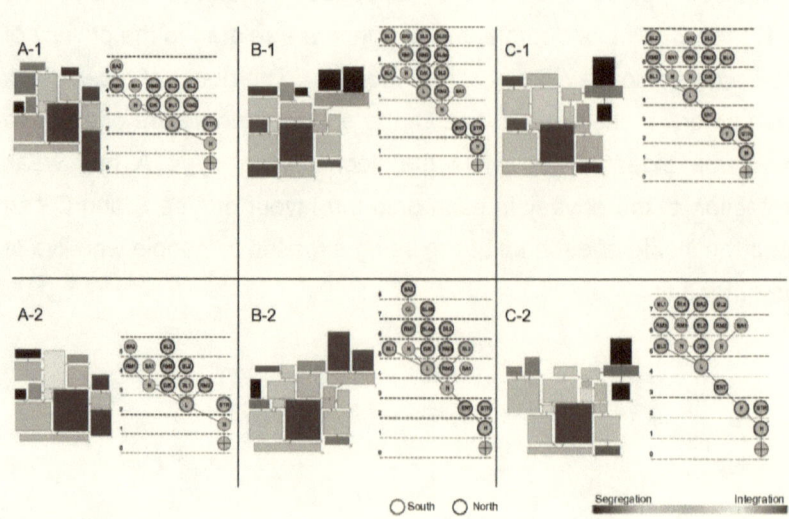

Figure 4 Convex maps and J-graphs of Unit Plans3

play the role of the center space of the life in the units. This result is also similar to the previous research that showed living and dining-kitchen spaces originated from the courtyard of the traditional Korean urban housing and these spaces are a central space in the housing (Choi, 1999; □□□ Kang et al., 1999).

Second, the depth of type A is narrower than type B and C, and the mean integration values of type A are higher than those of type B and C (Table 2). In addition, the numbers of convex in the units of type B and C are greater than those in the unit of type A. While the widths of unit size in type B and C (three bay widths) are larger than those in type A (two bay widths), the spaces in these B and C types become more segregated.

---

3 L – living space; D/K – dining & kitchen space; RM – bedroom; BA – bathroom; BL – balcony; STR – stair; H – hall; N – node space

unit	integration of major spaces in each unit(descending order)							
A-1	L	D/K	RM2		RM1	BA1	RM3	BA2
	2.312357	1.600862	1.095327		0.945964	0.867134	0.832448	0.612094
A-2	L	D/K		RM1	RM2	RM3	BA1	BA2
	2.081121	1.734268		0.945964	0.945964	0.945964	0.867134	0.612094
B-1	L		D/K	RM2	BA1	RM1	RM3	BA2
	1.472535		0.955158	0.841449	0.803201	0.803201	0.768279	0.579358
B-2	L	D/K		RM3	RM2	BA1	RM1	BA2
	1.536558	1.104401		0.930022	0.861972	0.82188	0.803201	0.465011
C-1	L	D/K		RM1	RM3	RM2	BA1	BA2
	1.613319	1.195051		0.80666	0.786985	0.733327	0.701443	0.576186
C-2	L	D/K		RM1	RM3	RM2	BA1	BA2
	1.413633	1.009738		0.785352	0.751933	0.692958	0.666808	0.570014

Table 1 Comparison of Integration Values of Spaces

unit		Depth	Integration	South	Middle	North
A-1	mean	3.00	1.082478	1.241740	1.031063	1.006483
A-2	mean	3.07	1.059683	1.166689	1.012676	1.021085
B-1	mean	4.53	0.796192	0.859585	0.870245	0.702365
B-2	mean	4.47	0.830410	0.938915	0.889528	0.737287
C-1	mean	4.61	0.840446	0.939881	0.823247	0.792849
C-2	mean	4.47	0.772689	0.852353	0.825607	0.711690

20% higher

Table 2 Comparison of Depth and Integration values

Third, the mean integration values in the southern part are higher than those values in the northern part in each unit plan if those living spaces be oriented to the south. In addition, the median integration values in the southern part of each unit are also higher than those in the northern part: Type A-1, 0.97>0.83; Type A-2, 0.95=0.95; Type B-1, 0.82>0.69; Type B-2, 0.86>0.71; Type C-1, 0.81>0.75; Type C-2, 0.75>0.67. Thus, the integration values seem to be related to the spatial orientation in these units, in which spatially integrated spaces are located in the southern part.

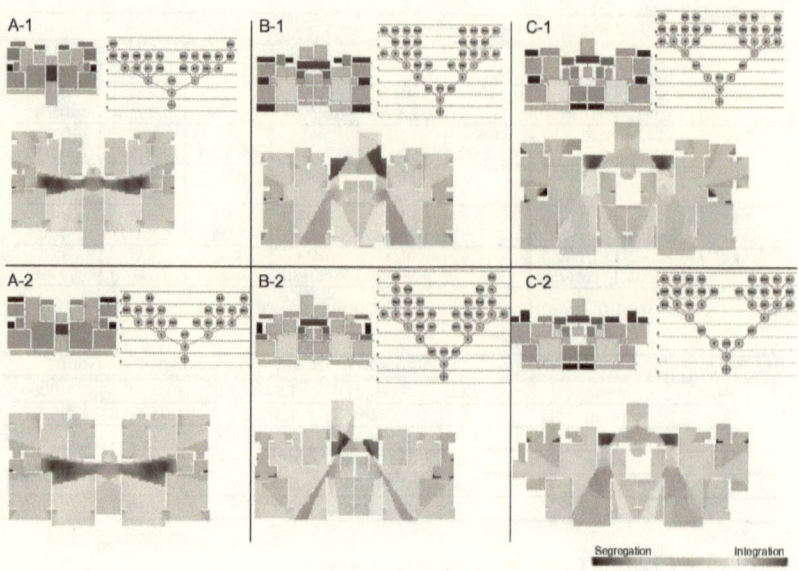

Figure 5 Convex maps, J-graphs, and Visual Integration maps of Floor Plans

First, hall spaces between two units have the highest integration value in these floor plans while living spaces have the highest value in the unit plans. Comparing Figure 4 and 5, the most integrated space moves from the living space to the hall space. When the boundary of the spatial analysis is only a unit plan, living space is the highest. However, when the boundary includes both the other unit plan and the hall space for the analysis of floor plans, hall spaces become the highest. Thus, the hall space is the center space in the floor plans while living space is the center space in the unit plans.

Second, the patterns of integration values seem to change from type A to type B, and then from type B to type C. Focusing on the highest integration values, in the hall spaces, the most integrated spaces penetrate into living spaces of two units in type A. However, the patterns of the highest integration values are located only in those hall spaces of type B and type C, and do not penetrate into living spaces.

In these patterns, the problems of privacy can occur in the hall space between two units. In order to keep privacy from being exposed to the other side, the change of those integration patterns can be an issue in the spatial configuration. Thus, according to those patterns, in type B and type C, the privacy of living spaces can be more protected from the outside of those units than the privacy in type A.

In addition, the distances between highly integrated spaces in the hall space of type C is greater than those of type B (Figure 5 and 6). The hall space of type C reduces exposure to other residents in the hall. Therefore, in terms of the protection of privacy in each unit on the floor plan, the unit and floor design have been developed to improve privacy to be less exposed to the public spaces and the other units.

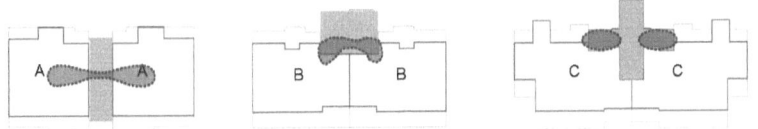

Figure 6 Changes in the most integrated spaces of these floor plans

INTERPRETATION

Changes in unit plans seek to maintain the preference of space: center-located living space and south-oriented bedrooms. As two bay-width unit plans have been improved toward three bay-width unit plans, more bedrooms have been located to the southern part and are able to get southern daylight. Because Korea is located in the northern latitude and its climate is in the Temperate Zone, the southern facing space is more compatible than the northern facing spaces for the domestic space. More bedrooms are designed to have southern orientation in the early 2000s. In addition, the means of integration values of southern spaces are greater than the means of integration values of northern spaces. In terms of designing spaces facing south, the means of integration values seem to be correlated to the socio-cultural context of the preference of southern orientation in the Korea apartment housing.

Changes in floor plans seek to enhance the privacy of space. Serving many units on the same floor, the hall space becomes integrated space. When the domestic spaces, such as units, are more linked to the hall space in the floor plan, this linking space will have the higher value. Thus, these linking spaces like the hall produce the problem of privacy between both units. In this situation, these linking spaces need to be designed to protect the privacy of each unit. For more private circumstances, the highly integrated area needs to be more separated from each other in these linking spaces. The way to distribute integrated spaces in the linking space is related to the level of privacy in each domestic space of the Korea apartment housing.

CONCLUSION

The design of Korean apartment housing in terms of a floor plan seeks to enhance the privacy of each unit maintaining the common characteristics of each unit space as a domestic space. First, the preference of southern orientation can explain the change in unit plans of the Korean apartment, which are wider width and have more southern oriented bedrooms. This preference can be a common characteristic of the Korean apartment. Second, linking spaces in the floor plan like a hall are designed for getting a wide distribution of integrated spaces in order to keep the privacy of each unit in the same floor. Therefore, the spatial analysis of Korean apartment housing explains ways to design an apartment unit for a better living place in terms of accepting residents' preference and keeping privacy of space.

Living in an apartment building usually shows that residents would share common spaces and would have more socialized characteristics rather than living in an single detached housing. However, in Korea, an apartment unit has been developed to enhance privacy in resident's domestic place. Apartment design has been approached to give each unit its own semi-private space. Each unit seeks to enclose its own buffer space from a public area. People who live in a building type that could easily share space with others actually want to live in another privatized building type that keeps their space from others who live in the same building. In fact, apartment housing in Korea is another type of a single privatized house but with the shape of vertical stack of units, which was the conventional view of an apartment as a socialized housing type.

However, this result from the research question is insufficient for generalization. This study analyzes small numbers of selected Korean apartment housing. Some results can explain the relation between the change in apartment and the social and cultural characteristics in Korea. This study seeks to introduce characteristics of Korean apartment housing, and analyze changes in design of these apartment plans. Thus, for future studies, some research questions and topics can be considered based on this study. One of the issues is whether metric dimension changes in width and depth of the unit plan are related to the spatial change in apartment housing. Another is whether people who live in apartment housing want to have a more private space or to have a more socialized space in an apartment building. In addition, because Korean apartment housing has been constructed as apartment estates, researchers seek to include analyses of the relationship between apartment buildings as well as a single floor in an apartment building in order to explain how the allocation of apartment buildings are correlated to socio-cultural characteristics in Korea.

References

Amorim, L. (1997). The Sector Paradigm. *Proceedings of the First International Space Syntax Conference*(2), 18.11-18.14.

Amorim, L. (2001). House of Recife: From diachrony to synchrony. *Proceedings of the Third International Space Syntax Conference*, 19.11-19.16.

Angel, S. (2000). *Housing Policy Matters: a global analysis*. New York: Oxford U Press.

Choi, J. (1999). The traditional characteristics reflected in the plan of modern apartment houses in Korea. *Journal of Architectural and Planning Research, 16*(1), pp.65-77.

Hanson, J. (1998). *Decoding Homes and Houses*: Cambridge Unversity Press.

Hillier, B. (1996). *Space is the machine : a configurational theory of architecture* Cambridge ; New York, NY, USA: Cambridge University Press.

Hillier, B., & Hanson, J. (1984). *The social logic of space*. Cambridge [Cambridgeshire] ; New York: Cambridge University Press.

Lara, F. L., & Kim, Y. (forthcoming). Built global, lived local: a study of how two diametrically opposed cultures reacted to similar modern housing solutions. *Journal of Architectural and Planning Research.*

Monteiro, C. (1997). Activity Analysis in Houses of Recife, Bazil. *Proceedings of the First International Space Syntax Conference*(2), 20.21-20.13.

Kang, B.-S., Kang, I.-H., Park, G.-J., Park, I.-S., Park, C.-S. Bak, H.-S., et al. (1999). *History of Apartments in Korea.* □□ Seoul: □□□ Sejin Book.

Korean Statistical Information Service (Publication. (2007). from Korea National Statistical Office: http://www.kosis.kr/

Choi, J.-P., Cho, H.-K., Park, I.-S., & Park, Y.-S. (2004). - 1966~2002- A Spatial Analysis of the Apartment Unit Plans from 1966 to 2002 in Seoul. *Journal of Architectural Institute of Korea, 20*(6), 155-164.

Spatial Changes in Bombay's gated communities.

Transformações espaciais em condomínios fechados de Bombay.

Romil Sheth

As rápidas transformações na sociedade Indiana a partir dos anos 90 criaram uma nova classe media cujas demandas espaciais são o foco do trabalho de doutorado de Romil Sheth. Neste texto o autor explica as origens do termo nova-classe-média e suas repercussões no espaço da cidade de Bombay (Mumbai), em espacial o fenômeno dos condomínios fechados. Como parte do Global Apartments Research Group o autor estudou dezenas de novos empreendimentos em Bombay e fez 20 entrevistas com residentes em 2006. O texto que segue é resultado parcial deste trabalhoe revela questões interessantíssimas, principalmente quando se pensa em fenômenos paralelos no Brasil. O componente religioso da exclusão por exemplo se revela uma grande diferença enquanto que a violência urbana praticamente inexiste na Índia apesar da desigualdade. No entanto, a mesma percepção da cidade como algo caótico, ameaçador e incontrolável alimenta o discurso por trás do isolamento do condomínio fechado. No interior das unidades, a ocorrência de duas cozinhas, uma toda linda para os donos da casa se exibirem e outra para o preparo cotidiano dos alimentos pelos empregados, remete imediatamente ao caso brasileiro.

An examination of the contemporary landscape of Bombay reveals a distinct pattern in which real estate development has shifted in a significant manner from the traditional downtown precinct of South Bombay to the northern and eastern fringes of the mainland in areas traditionally considered to be 'suburbs'. Within South and Central Bombay, the majority of new developments are linked to processes of gentrification and urban renewal, especially within the dense vernacular fabric of the 'native town'[1]. At a superficial level, the nature of these typologies seem similar to typical building archetypes of the mixed use residential tower, the gated community, the multiplex and the urban shopping mall. Most projects have very strong references and characteristics with similar developments in SE Asian countries such as Singapore, Honk Kong and Malaysia and are often designed by firms from these countries. However, a pilot project[2] that I carried out during the summer of 2006 seems to suggest that while new residential and commercial buildings can be traced back to familiar archetypes, there maybe something very distinct and particular about the nature of these typologies that are being developed in Bombay. My interest lies in examining the nature of these new developments and broader processes of urban development in Mumbai to explore the various factors leading to the

---

[1] The term 'Native Town' was used by the Colonial Administration to refer to the local Indian population and was separated from the Colonial Fort by a series of large open spaces known as maidans. Currently this area is characterized by 4-5 storey tall buildings with an extremely high population density primarily comprising of the lower middle class and the working classes. The book, Bombay-Cities Within by Mehrotra and Dwivedi presents an extensive historical account of the native town and its evolution.

[2] The pilot project was carried out from May 2006-August 2006 in Bombay where I spent time collecting primary information in the form of plans of new developments, photographing them and conducting informal interviews with real estate developers. I also, conducted a series of 20 interviews through extensive questionnaires as part of the Global Apartments Research Project; the data of which was subsequently collated and analyzed. This analysis presents some interesting insights and are extremely pertinent to my research as will be described later in this paper..

generation of these building typologies. A primary intention being to determine the extent to which these typologies are distinct and particular to Mumbai and their implication on the transformation of traditional relationships between the 'home' and the 'public realm.' These questions are not merely about real estate dynamics and the creation of new physical form but instead represent a highly complex issue that requires the examination of a set of closely intertwined processes such as the nature of representation and promotion of these developments in print and televised advertisements, the impact of federal neo-liberal policies, global capital flows and the role of the state in urban development, broader changes in the social constitution of the middle class and its symbolism, and, the impact of new attitudes towards consumerism and lifestyle production. While I will outline some of the major arguments related to these questions, this paper will primarily focus on types of 'gated' developments in Bombay.

The construction frenzy in Mumbai over the last decade has been accompanied by an equally intense campaign for marketing and promoting new projects through large hoardings, televised and printed material, brochures and frequent publications dedicated to various aspects of the real estate industry. The representation of individual projects in this material is particularly intriguing.

An interesting aspect of these advertisements is the manner in which the same descriptive language is employed regardless of the scale and type of development. Whether its individual apartment buildings, small clusters of residential buildings or a large township the manner of representation begins to suggest a number of fundamental characteristics that are common to each of these new developments. A primary emphasis is the creation of a new clean and healthy environment equipped with a number of facilities and amenities of 'international standard' that make these developments clearly different from the 'city' which is portrayed as being crowded, polluted and chaotic. Another major issue associated with common perceptions of the city is the assurance of a high level of security and safety within the development. The various depictions in these advertisements also imply that these projects are aimed at creating a distinct 'lifestyle' for a very a specific target audience - often referred to as 'the global Indian'[3]

A number of scholarly studies,[4] which need to be examined in greater detail suggest that the complicated caste and class structure of contemporary Indian society makes the definition the 'global Indian' a highly controversial and contested subject. However, most commonly the agency of the 'global Indian' can be ascribed to specific segments of the urban middle class in India that are fluent in English, predominantly employed in the service sector agency and indulge in relatively high levels of consumerism. Commentators refer to this group as the 'new middle class', 'modern middle class' or the 'new rich'. Leela Fernandes in her study on the 'Rise of the New Middle Class in Liberalizing India points out that, "The invention of the new middle class in the context of economic liberalization thus involves a discursive production of a new cultural image of the Indian middle class rather than the entry of a new social group to this class. In this

---

[3] The term 'middle class' in the Indian context creates the perception of the working class and though by academic categorization most people in Bombay can be stratified into segments of the middle class, a majority of people who would normally be termed as the upper middle class would refuse to be associated with this terminology and would prefer to be termed as simply the upper class. This may also be representative of deeper class and caste based hierarchies that are deeply embedded in Indian Society?

[4] A Number of scholarly studies focusing on different countries in SE Asia have been devoted to examining recent transformations in culture and social practices as a result of processes of globalization. In the Indian case there are significant works by Arjun Appadurai, Rachel Dwyer, Sanjay Joshi, William Mazerella, Anthony King, etc

process, the new (urban) Indian middle class becomes a central agent for the re-visioning of the Indian nation in the context of globalization" (Fernandes, 2006). Thus this social group is not only considered symbolic to the potential benefits of India's integration with the global economy but has also come to represent a new ideal of 'Indianness.'

This popular perception is not only supported by the representation of their practices, desires and aspirations in various forms of media (advertisements, televised soap operas, Bollywood films, etc) but also by a number of statistical surveys by independent consultancy firms that present almost implausible figures about their growth patterns and income levels. For instance this recent survey by the McKinsey[5] group speculates that by 2025, the middle class will grow from current estimates of 50 million to 583 million!

"Along with the shift from rural to urban consumption, India will witness the rapid growth of its middle class – households with disposable incomes from 200,000 to 1,000,000 rupees a year. That class now comprises about 50 million people, roughly 5% of the population. By 2025 a continuing rise in personal incomes will spur a tenfold increase, enlarging the middle class to about 583 million people, or 41% of the population. In 20 years the shape of the income pyramid will have become unrecognizable. The Indian middle class

---

[5] The McKinsey group is a global consultancy firm that specializes in market analysis as one of their core competencies. Along with other groups such as Ernst and Young and Arthur Anderson they are actively involved in preparing various documents that report on lifestyle trends to consumer habits to real estate development potentials. They are often hired by large real estate developers, prospective financial investors and in some cases even by the Indian Government. While there seems to be a particular research methodology used for data collation and analysis in these reports it is seldom described with the data being primarily presented in the form of dramatic statements used to capture the readers attention

has already begun to evolve, and by 2025 it will dominate the cities."
(McKinsey, 2006)

At another level these perceptions also seem to be reinforced and in accordance with the neo-liberal policies of the central government who has since 'liberalization' consciously shifted from its previous socialist agenda to focus on large scale infrastructure projects (development of bridges, roads, expressways, installation of high speed data cables, tele-communication networks, etc) and the creation of a conducive environment for attracting foreign investment and effectively managing flows of capital. Simultaneously, the city has also assembled a taskforce of local elites, corporate leaders and politicians known as Bombay First to "prioritize and plan for land development, housing, and economic development activities in order to improve the city's global standing and 'make Mumbai a world class city by 2013" (State of Maharashtra, 2004). For Bombay their primary vision is of transforming the city into a clean, efficient, 'world class' financial center with the popular metaphorical reference being of transforming 'Bombay into Shanghai.' It is interesting to point out that during the first waves of economic liberalization in the 1990's the primary reference was Singapore whose high levels of civic hygiene, efficiency of state institutions and the maintenance of a consistently high standard living, all set within a tropical landscape was often referred to as the overall aspiration for the city. The recent shift of reference to Shanghai is significant in that it is reflective of the slow pace of reforms in Mumbai and aimed at demonstrating the scale and pace with which a city in a similar regional context (South Asia) can be transformed into a 'global commercial capital'. This attitude is emblematic of a singular vision by city planners and politicians where the radical transformation of the physical form is perceived as being fundamental to transforming Mumbai into a 'Global City' and warding off competition for foreign investment from other rapidly developing smaller urban centers in India (Bangalore, Chennai, Hyderabad).

This vision is also representative of growing disparity levels within the city where the uneven nature of contemporary urban development is contributing in significant ways in creating a pattern similar to a classic industrial class structure similar to many other cities in SE Asia in which security manned walled enclaves seal off lifestyles of consumerism and luxury from the urban poor and the working classes. Arjun Appadurai articulates, "the rich in these cities seek to gate as much of their lives as possible, traveling from guarded homes to darkened cars to air conditioned offices, moving always in an envelope of privilege through the heat of public poverty and the dust of dispossession" (Appadurai, 2000). In the case of Mumbai this phenomenon is particularly acute as approximately 60%[6] of the city's population constitutes of pavement dwellers and slum inhabitants who do not have access to formal housing. The proliferation of informal housing and the displacement of the urban poor in a climate of continual economic growth makes it even more disturbing and can be attributed to a politics of forgetting which has been articulated by Gavin Shatkin as a 'loss of institutional memory'. Shatkin points out that, "the new policy agenda has resulted in a 'loss of institutional memory' regarding the settlements of the poor, as the rhetoric of economic growth and prosperity for all through incorporation into the global economy masks the reality of shelter poverty" (Shatkin, 2004).

---

[6] Census figures in India is a highly political and contentious issue as has been analyzed by a numerous scholarly studies. In the case of Bombay the large amount of population living in informal settlements has apparently not been mapped and a figure of 50-70% is thrown around to illustrate the numbers that do not have access to formal housing

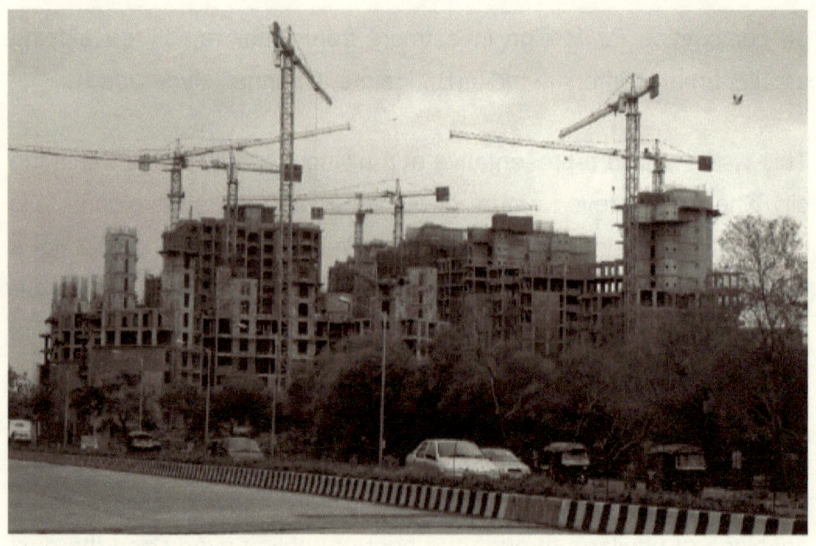

New construction in NE Bombay suburbs

A resultant of these processes has been the recent spate of 'cleaning up' and 'urban beautification' projects in the form of historic preservation of buildings, redevelopment of urban spaces and slum relocation schemes to allow for the insertion of new infrastructure and to open up valuable real estate sites from slum aggregations for market rate developments. While these projects play an essential part in the development and growth of the city they are largely determined by the politics of real estate dynamics to the extent that the emerging form of the city now seems to be largely governed by the processes of the private sector rather than by planning and urban design professionals. Also, the apparent lack of a regulatory framework by the State that would normally help guide such development has led to significant conflicts with already established land use and the positioning of new infrastructure. This condition where zoning policies, land use master plans, transportation planning and other forms of civic infrastructure often have no relationships with each other and are easily subverted leads to a number of moral issues regarding the nature of contemporary urban development in the city and raises a fundamental question: Is the city being hijacked by the practices of specific social groups who perceive themselves as 'proper citizens' and seek to exclude others - namely the urban poor?

A number of scholarly studies[7] also argue that the resultant unprecedented exposure to lifestyles of wealthy foreign countries through advertising, televised serials and popular culture coupled with rising incomes and the influx of western goods into the market has subsequently led to the widespread consumption of luxury and semi-luxury goods. This increase in consumerism is however, not restricted to certain segments of society such as the upper and wealthier middle classes but is also evidenced amongst the larger middle class and the lower classes though in a relatively lesser degree. Given the highly pluralistic nature of Indian society, who constitutes the middle class? What are its boundaries? What is the nature of 'consumption' and how does it differ from their counterparts in other parts of SE Asia? form highly complicated and often controversial issues which are not directly addressed in most studies. Instead recent scholarship has employed different parameters such as education, income, occupation, etc to determine the size and nature of the urban middle class. Despite this a number of recent surveys have placed the population of the middle class in India as being anywhere from 50 million to 300 million people out of a total population of one billion (NCAER, 1994; Varma, 1998; ORG-Marg and Media Users Research Group, 2001)

---

[7] Refer to works by Anthony King, Chua Beng Huat, Michael Pinches, Salim Lakha, Carol Breckenridge, etc that present extensive argumentation on these aspects in both the Indian condition as well as other countries in SE Asia

The existing landscape of residential development in south and central Bombay reveals a distinct juxtaposition of tall high rise towers with a squatter settlement sprawling at its base. Even in posh neighborhoods within the city the presence of the urban poor who establish their dwellings in interstitial spaces is hard to ignore. A large part of the population that resides in these slums is often directly employed as domestic help in the plush residential towers that surround them and despite several attempts to rid these neighborhoods of slums they still proliferate. Arjun Appadurai presents an interesting insight into this phenomenon; "as domestic servants, they often have small rooms in the large apartment buildings of the rich, and these servants often bring friends and dependents, who spill out into the stairwells, the enclosed compounds, and the foyers. The official tenants, owners, and landlords wage a constant war against this colonization from below, but it is frequently lost because - as in all societies based on financial apartheid-one wants the poor near at hand as servants but far away as humans" (Appadurai, 2002).

As a number of advertisements and marketing material reveals, the ubiquitous presence of slums, the frequent colonization of public spaces by hawkers and the destitute and the high density levels in the city are constantly being manipulated by real estate developers to create a general perception of the city as being unhygienic, unsafe and chaotic. As Gyan Prakash writes, "To the elites the city appears under siege, imperiled by spatial mutations and occupation by the uncivil masses, a wasteland of broken modernist dreams. Bombay is now "slumbay," say the elites." Thus it is not surprising that advertisements for contemporary residential developments emphasize the creation of new environments endowed with clean 'crisp air', large green spaces, and 'exquisitely landscaped gardens' as an escape from the unhealthy, degraded environment of the city –

'far removed from the city's bustle and pollution, maddening traffic and swarming crowds.' The vision of this new environment is suggestive of the creation of a distinct biosphere, far away from the city where even the air one breathes is different - 'cleaner, purer and invigorating.'

Another central element vigorously marketed in contemporary developments is that of a 'particular lifestyle'. At one level this takes on the form of an aspirational character which is largely in alignment with broader narratives of adopting a 'global lifestyle' that is characterized by the presence of an array of luxury amenities such as spas, health clubs, etc that are designed according to 'international standards.' At another level these processes of lifestyle production have also led to a "polities of exclusion" at the level of the city; a driving force that seeks to sanitize public spaces in the city in order to render them acceptable to a certain standard imposed by particular segments of the middle class population. This is evidenced in the proliferation of a number of gated communities as a model of contemporary residential development followed by several attempts by the state and private organizations to purge Mumbai's public spaces of squatters and encroachers in an attempt reclaim these spaces for the use of 'proper citizens'. Questioning these practices as being representative of a 'global bourgeois vision of 21st century urbanity'; Partha Chatterjee points out that," In metropolis after Indian metropolis, organized civic groups have come forward to demand from the administration and the judiciary that laws and regulations for the proper use of land, public spaces and thoroughfares be formulated and strictly adhered to in order to improve the quality of life of citizens. Everywhere the dominant cry seems to be to rid the city of encroachers and polluters and, as it were, to give the city back to its proper citizens" (Chatterjee, 2004).

In tension with the ideology of creating a distinct lifestyle and status based on consumption is the practice of gentrification and the development of a broader pattern of state sponsored privatization. This manifests in two distinct forms of urban development. The first results in the 'upgrading' of existing neighborhoods by inserting new leisure and lifestyle amenities such as malls, restaurants, supermarkets, etc as well as radical changes in the facades and lobbies of existing buildings through the use of granite and marble, materials perceived to be representative of upper class status., Ranjani Mazumdar observes "Despite the coexistence of wealth and poverty cheek by jowl throughout Bombay's physical topography, the redesigning of the interiors provides an escape from the chaotic experience of the street just outside. Capitalist modernity has historically required a regime of spatial aesthetics that can house and generate the magic of the commodity. In this situation the transformation of the interior provides the fleeting possibility of transcending the physical texture of the cityscape."

The second manifests itself in the form of urban space 'beautification' projects where the state has in the past decade actively tried to 'clean' urban spaces of hawkers and the urban poor. This process of sanitization can be viewed as another process of the politics of exclusion resulting from the very high population density of the city and the intense contestation over pubic space in the city.

Gated Residential Developments in Mumbai

"Gated communities,' or 'fortified enclaves,' are privatized, enclosed, and monitored spaces for residence, consumption, leisure, and work" (Caldeira 1999).

The development of a number of gated residential projects on the fringes of the city and yet within close proximity of major lifestyle, consumer and work facilities seem to be in direct response to some of the issue outlined above. As commentators have noted this phenomenon is also reflective of a broader issue pertaining to large urban conglomerations or 'mega cities' such as Mumbai, where the state in its continual struggle to provide adequate infrastructure and services at the core leads to the creation of a general impression that the standard of living within the main city is rapidly deteriorating despite the high income taxes and prices paid for prime real estate. According to Robert Fishman this is not a new phenomenon and can be historically traced to, "early industrial cities of the North of England in the first half of the nineteenth-century, where the bourgeoisie escaped the rapidly-deteriorating conditions of the core to settle in gated villa communities like "Victoria Park" in Manchester. There the factory owners and wealthy professionals could buy for themselves the services and security available nowhere else in this first industrial "shock city" and create a green, healthy, well-protected "environment of privilege" at the edge". (Fishman, 1989)

The astronomical rise in property prices in South and Central Bombay from the 1980's has led to a significant change in population demographic with a clear shift noticeable towards suburban areas such as Andheri, Jogeshwari, Kandivali, Juhu, Versova, Powai, Mulund and Malad. While population in these areas has grown by 50% between 1981 and 1991, the population in south and central

Bombay has gradually declined. This loss of population can also be explained by the fact that many middle class families who lived in small apartments in this part of the city sold their property for significant profits and moved to new developments in the suburbs where they could easily purchase larger and more lavish forms of accommodation (Patel, 2005). This population shift is significant, because it is in these suburbs that contemporary residential and commercial development in the city is concentrated in and continues at a frenetic pace.

In Bombay the development of enclosed housing developments can be historically traced to colonial British enclaves and the 'blocks of flats' specially designed to house public officials that worked in the Railways, Customs and Public Works department. These developments were highly introverted in character, enclosed by a high wall and designed to create a sanitized environment in reaction to the increasing pollution, density and noise of the city. At this juncture it should also be emphasized that enclosed residential development have a much deeper historical lineage that can be traced back to vernacular urban neighborhoods in different parts of the country. For instance the concept of the 'mohalla' or 'pol' as an ethno-linguistic neighborhood (Gillion, 1968) that traditionally housed only a specific religious or communal group is a common feature of the traditional Indian cities. These neighborhoods though not 'gated' in the sense of an enclosure wall created a physical boundary by having the rear walls of every house organized to segregate it from the adjoining neighborhood (Gillion, 1968). Also each traditional neighborhood had a well defined gateway that marked access points to it. In this manner these vernacular enclosed residential developments challenge the notion that gated developments in contemporary India are not purely a resultant of a global phenomenon of an increase in gated developments based on the popular American model and at least in the Indian context have deeper historical roots.

The primary distinction between contemporary gated communities being developed in the northern suburbs of Bombay and older vernacular types is the degree and intensity of their introverted character. As Fazlon points out, while a "colony" usually refers to residential units and the social interaction that goes with them, the new developments broaden the interactive field (even as they restrict it to the few) and offer a lifestyle wherein residents do not merely reside but live within the protective walls" (Falzon, 2004). Most gated developments are marketed as offering a number of facilities that range from an extensive security system to 'manicured gardens' in smaller developments to extensive parks, swimming pools, designated children play areas, health facilities to even hi-the security systems. As described in the following advertisement, these developments are aimed at relocating aspects of daily life that are usually enacted in urban public spaces to within a private, fortified zone.

"Set amid 72 acres of pristine natural environs, Lodha Paradise is far removed from the city's bustle and pollution. The air here is crisp and invigorating and you feel a liberating sense of space in the extensively green and sprawling surroundings. This self-contained township features a Ganesha Temple, world class ICSE School, exquisite landscaped gardens, excellent sports & recreational facilities, Olympic-sized swimming pool, Crèche/ Day-care center and an international shopping mall within its precincts. Designed for the upwardly mobile, Lodha Paradise is Thane's finest residential development, celebrating unparalleled luxury amid the beautiful natural locale. Come and discover your own piece of paradise at Thane's premiere residential township - Lodha Paradise!"

A seminal study on gated communities in the United States done by E. Blakely and J. Synder define gated or master planned communities as presenting, "the home buyer with 'a complete package'. Housing developers are faced with the need to sell more than the shelter. They market not just homes in a carefully planned environment, but a total living experience. This is the new town as lifestyle. As reflected in advertising and the complexity of design and amenities, the commodity they are selling is not just houses, but a community" (Blakely and Snyder, 1999). Further, they point out that gated community developments can be categorized into three distinct models; lifestyle communities, prestige communities, and security zone communities. 'Lifestyle communities' are identified as those that market a specific form of living as a complete 'package', such as golf course communities, retirement communities, etc. "Prestige communities are the exclusive enclaves for the rich, famous or upper middle class people. They tend to show the prestige of the community, the image is the main focus thus the gate defines the barrier of status. Finally, Security Zone communities are the ones created by the dwellers not by the developer". Within Mumbai however, the characteristics of these three types are often found combined into one cohesive gated development and vigorously marketed as constituting a 'total lifestyle solution.'

Within contemporary India, gated communities were initially developed to exclusively cater to Non-Resident Indians that were part of the Indian diaspora (NRI) with the marketing strategy that it followed 'international standards' both in terms of its aesthetics as well as the provision of amenities (swimming pool, lush gardens, health club, etc). The construction of these projects was also representative of liberal economic policies which allowed large amounts of direct foreign investment into these projects as a result of the significant difference in exchange rate between India and other

Euro-American countries (King, 2004). The increase in housing demand in the past decade, the association of these projects with a particular 'international' lifestyle that is in alignment with the lifestyles and aspirations of the new urban middle class, assurance of safe and secure environment and their provision of a number of amenities (primarily unhindered water and electricity and leisure and recreation facilities) that the city is unable to provide have led this typology to become the preferred model of development for most large scale residential projects in the city. Also, their location on cheaper land far away from the city core makes them relatively affordable and hence immensely attractive.

The development of these projects is also closely linked to a number of structural transformations taking place within the constitution of the urban middle class. The practices and outlooks of the new urban middle class have been instrumental in a fundamental questioning of the prevailing manner of urban living, reforming existing conceptions of the 'good life' and gradually destabilizing existing social structures within the 'traditional Indian' household. As age old distinctions within the Indian home are questioned the position of the middle class woman has acquired enormous significance and emerges as a set of contradictory images. In a recent study of the new middle class in Mumbai, Tim Scrase points out that, "The gains from women under neo-liberal reforms have been regarded as resulting from an enlightened outlook of, and cultural changes within families together with a range of ongoing political initiatives. Despite rising salaries and employment in male dominated high status jobs where the ideology of 'togetherness 'prevail; women do not seek to be autonomous beings, separate from their households nor is such a proposition socially acceptable" (Scrase, 2006). 'The New Indian Woman' as the publicity release for a contemporary women's magazine puts it is "the tough as nails career woman who finds it easy to indulge in the occasional superstition. Her outlook is global, but her values would make her grandma proud."[8] Another significant aspect is the rapidly growing number of women entering the traditionally male dominated workforce which has not only created dual income families that can actively participate in the production of new lifestyles but has also posed a serious challenge to existing older notions of domesticity and urban living. This has been further compounded by the increasing break-up of traditional multi-generational joint family households and the proliferation of single family households (Nijman, 2006). A phenomenon well represented by the presence of a large number of one bedroom apartments in new developments accompanied by crèches and day care amenities.

Security and surveillance form another critical factor in the selection of neighborhoods and residential developments to live in. This need for a high level of security and protection is borne out of fear from three broad patterns of violence that are embedded in the minds of the general population in the city. First is the strong sense of apprehension created by the increased presence of the underworld, as evidenced in numerous stories of extortion and periodic terrorization of private citizens.

Second, is the fear of communal violence which has emerged in the past decade as a highly disturbing trend and which continues to surface periodically in a number of cities in the country. Despite the heterogeneous constitution of the city, the fear of communal violence

---

[8] This quote aptly describes contemporary Indian society's attitude towards women wherein despite changing sensibilities they are still regarded as the primary guardians of tradition, culture and values interesting manifestations of this paradox are often physically manifested in contemporary apartment design that is described later in the paper

is largely a result of the post Babri Masjid[9] demolition riots that took place in the city between December 1992 and January 1993, leaving approximately 800 people dead. This event has been hard to erase from collective memory partly due to its extremely violent nature and partly due to the imposing presence of the Shiv Sena, a fundamentalist Hindu political party that ardently advocates cleansing the city of all 'Muslim Invaders' (Thomas Blom Hansen, 1991). Gyan Prakash articulates, "Described as "de-cosmpolitisation" and "provincialisation," the Sena's attempt to replace universal citizenship with exclusivist regional and communal conditions for rights tot eh city is ironically related to globalization's growing presence in Bombay. Both have arisen on the ruins of the modernist projects. The destruction of the industrial city and radical working class politics, the dismantling of the post-colonial developmentalist state ad the shattering of the dreams of universal citizenship and social equality have set the context for the rise of both the ethnic particularism of the Shiv Sena and the globalization of capital. In place of the cosmopolitan and secular-nationalist modern city, Bombay's residents are now asked to embrace the exclusivist ideology of regionalism and Hindu chauvinism."

The spatial implications of this fear can be attributed to the number of new ethno-religious based enclaves that are being developed as well as a significant shift in demographics as a number of Muslim families have since the riots sold expensive real estate at extremely low prices in a desperate bid to move out of predominantly Hindu areas (Falzon,

---

[9] The Babri Masjid incident involves a long dispute between Hindus and Muslims over a site in Ayodhya that is currently a Masjid but has deep significance as a religious Hindu site. In December, 1992 the Masjid was ravaged by Hindu fundamentalists that was followed by a more organized attack a month later that also targeted Muslim homes and businesses. This incident sparked off a series of communal riots through different parts of the country. The riots in Bombay were particularly intense and had a profound effect on the city's populace

2004). The presence of a prominent Hindu shrine in new developments can be construed as being another aspect of this shift in attitude and the desire for creating homogeneous ethnic enclaves as a means of ensuring a safe and secure environment. Significantly, there do no seem to be any new developments that include a mosque or a church as an integral feature. Overall, these elements of violence have combined to instill a general feeling of fear and insecurity amongst the population resulting in a strong preference for properly secured and gated developments (Appadurai, 2000, Falzon, 2004).

Second is an increasing fear of violence perpetrated by servants and domestic help. Recent reports in newspapers about violent thefts, particularly of elderly folk, by servants has created a strong need for increased surveillance of domestic staff and the demand for providing separate spaces for them within the apartment complex that can be easily monitored. This has also resulted in the creation of an informal network amongst middle class citizens for the acquisition of 'trustworthy' domestic staff.

Thus practices of segregation are also maintained within the development between residents and the working classes, particularly domestic staff. This practice takes on an interesting form in these projects as manifested in the carefully orchestrated movement of service personnel (domestic staff, maintenance workers, etc) through the development by the provision of separate entrances, dedicated elevators and attached staff quarters in order to minimize their visibility and presence. The installation of extensive surveillance systems further helps monitor their activities in an effort to prevent any form of domestic violence. While this segregation is maintained to a large extent it gets subverted on frequent occasions and especially when maids accompany young children to the parks and playfields. In this case they not only travel via the same elevators as regular middle class residents but also occupy the same public spaces as them. Are the boundaries of exclusion in contemporary developments malleable and if so, then what determines the parameters and to what extent are they flexible?

Analyzing the various house plans shows a distinct spatial configuration wherein each function is clearly defined and enclosed. As the promotional material for this development asserts, "The need for privacy and modern style in the design is the most important factor". This sentiment is echoed in the individual house layout where a minimal transition space leads into a small receptacle off which a bedroom is placed. This bedroom near the entrance is designed to accommodate children or guests. While the living room retains its location at the center of the house its size has been greatly reduced with the additional area added to individual bedrooms. This additional area not only allows for significantly larger bedrooms replete with a seating space but also accommodates a large bathroom and walk-in closet. A significant feature is the presence of a television and music system in each individual room which forms an apt indicator of the need for 'own space' and 'own amenities' versus 'shared space' and 'shared amenities.'

evolution of the apartment plan

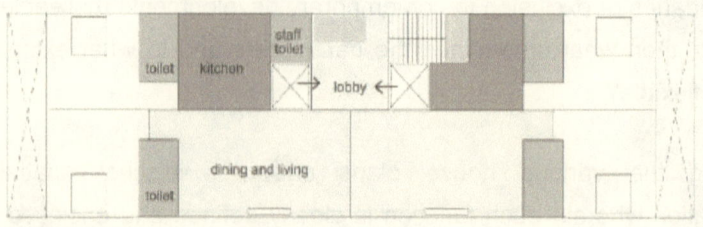

previous layout

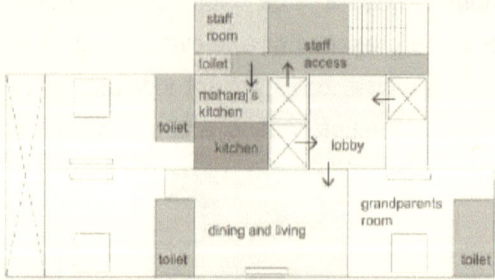

new layout - two bedroom apartment

new layout - one bedroom apartment

The surveys and subsequent analysis carried out for the Global Apartments Research project aptly indicate that a significant amount of time is spent by current residents in their bedrooms as opposed to common living spaces such as the dining room and the living room. As Ranjani Mazumdar states "Histories of consumer culture have shown how a withdrawal of the middle classes into their domestic interiors, electrical kitchens and private automobiles was required to enhance the experience of consumption. Interior design is central to the space of the familial and the private. Design techniques not only relate the interior to cultural forms, but also mark the space within a hierarchical chain of taste. Interior design also helps to negotiate personal identity, because it is the visible expression of our values and attitudes."

In this project, the practice of maintaining a clear segregation between the working classes and the upper class residents takes on an interesting form and is manifested in the carefully orchestrated movement of service personnel (domestic staff, maintenance workers, etc) through the development by the provision of separate entrances, dedicated elevators and attached staff quarters in order to minimize their visibility and presence. Within the development this articulation enables a clear separation of zones but more importantly allows the domestic staff to look after the house, especially young children in the absence of the parents. Here too, a significant addition is the creation of two separate kitchens within one house. The basic functional rationale being that the heavy and general cooking would usually be carried out by the domestic staff and is hence not a space that the woman should necessarily interact with. Also, this kitchen, often referred to as the 'Maharaj's Kitchen' is attached to the staff quarters and is used by the staff to prepare their food. Another aspect of this layout is that the entire zone can be closed off from the main house by a door in case of the family leaving the house for extended periods. The second kitchen often takes on the form of an open kitchen and is primarily used for garnishing and presenting food prepared in the second kitchen and often doubles up as a breakfast space. This kitchen is usually decorated with expensive appliances and finishes such as stainless steel and corian as opposed to the heavy cooking kitchen where local stones and granite are used. In effect the second kitchen which is also termed the 'women's kitchen' in a number of layouts is portrayed as an extension of the living and dining space and representative of the women's status in the house.

Also, the space given to thresholds or the creation of semi-public space is minimal; once again reiterating the need for a high degree of segregation. This manner of spatial planning is not a simplistic expression of a new manner of living but a manifestation of a system of complex relationships within the middle class home wherein social relationships are kept simultaneously intimate and yet, distant. Also, as the overall building plan shows, there are three distinct apartment types. While existing apartment buildings in the main city are characterized by a singular apartment type that caters to the multi-generational household new apartment buildings in gated communities, such as this one, are designed to cater to multiple family types - single family households, working professionals as well as multi-generational households. These subtle changes in interior layouts and apartment typologies signal a distinct shift taking place in attitudes toward the creation of the domestic realm with respect to changes in family structure and lifestyles that need to be examined in greater detail.

An interesting new type of residential development known as the 'vertical township' or the 'vertical gated community' has recently emerged, especially in dense inner areas of the city where limited space necessitates the need to build vertically. These residential towers form unique hybrids of the urban shopping mall and the gated community which are clearly evident in their physical form. The main entrance to the building is through a three storey structure which represents a mini-shopping mall replete with shops, a small supermarket, food court a games arcade and in some cases even a temple. The residential accommodation takes the form of a 20 – 30 storey vertical tower that is built on top and integrates a number of 'lifestyle' amenities found in regular gated developments such as a swimming pool, health club and gym, business center, landscaped terrace gardens, etc. This type of development signifies a distinctly new and innovative attitude towards creating segregated single residential towers especially in dense inner city neighborhoods where they stand juxtaposed with the chaos and frenzy of the local bazaar, street vendors and hawkers.

Essentially gated developments in Bombay creates a distinct residential environment in which the need for 'absolute privacy' and the desire for various services is celebrated to create a world of 'detachment and attachment, separation and connection' where similar to elite Indians in the colonial period the new global Indian resident has the choice of completely separating oneself from the rest of the city and interacting with it only when desired. Farha Ghannam in her examination of similar phenomenon in Cairo articulates these practices as a form of "'flexible urbanity,' that is, benefitting from city life while avoiding living in it. It means having access to all the sources and facilities linked to life in the city, yet, at the same time, being able to avoid its crowded streets, polluted air, and deteriorating infrastructure."

This raises an important question: Are gated communities simple a product of local circumstance, or are they global phenomena which happen to fit within a local context? It is important to note here that the conflicts and tensions being seen in contemporary Bombay are not unprecedented and nor are they an inevitable result of the numerous factors that were described above. Thus in the case of contemporary Bombay the rise of gated developments is not a derivative of purely causal factors but can also be ascribed to historical and contingent links by which elite residents in the city have sought to fortify their lives from the general public. Falzon also points out that, "It is important to overcome the global/local divide and to realize that gated communities make sense both in the global context and the production of a global architectural idiom, and in the local spatial context. Gated communities, to use Clifford's words for diasporas, are "always embedded in particular map; and histories" (Falzon, 2004)." Leisch makes an important distinction in his analysis of gated communities in Indonesia. In terms of style, he states that "they are a direct import from the US; with respect to junction, however, they accommodate the needs of Indonesian cities. Just as King's bungalow absorbed local meanings and idiosyncrasies as it spread, it would seem that gated communities worldwide do indeed share an origin and represent a global style of living in the contemporary world. Yet it is important to realize that they by no means constitute a homogenous field of meaning." (Leisch, 2002).

As these tensions and conflicts persist, and the city continues to grow and develop at a frenetic pace it is critical to create solutions that can help stem rapidly increasing disparity levels within the city. While the ideal solution to accommodate both, the aspirations and demands of the global middle class as well as the lower and working middle classes would be to significantly improve public infrastructure and the creation of well designed public spaces the tendency seems to be towards moving away from conflicting situations that the city throws up and retreating behind walled confines where its significantly easier to realize specific lifestyles and aspirations. At a broader level my primary interest lies in examining the transformation of the City and its perceptions with respect to a thorough analysis of emerging building typologies and changes in regulatory frameworks that are playing a significant role in shaping contemporary urbanism in the city. The goal would be to also establish a well grounded critique that could form the basis for the formation of a set of normative strategies or principles for contemporary planning and urban design in Bombay.

References:

Appadurai, Arjun – Spectral Housing and Urban Cleansing: Notes on Millennial Mumbai Public Culture 12 (3), 2000, pp 627-651

Banerjee-Guha, Swapna – Shifting Cities: Urban Restructuring in Mumbai Economic and Political Weekly, January 12 2002, pp 121-128

Blakely, E., and Synder, M - Fortress America: Gated Communities in the United States The Brookings Institution Press, MA 1997

Bourdieu, Pierre – Distinction: A Social Critique of the Judgment of Taste (trans. Richard Nice) Harvard Univ. Press, 2007

Breckenridge, Carol (ed.) – Consuming Modernity: Public Culture in a South Asian World Univ. of Minnesota Press, 1995

Chatterjee, Partha - Are Indian Cities Becoming Bourgeois at Last? Body. City, siting contemporary culture in India, House of World cultures, Berlin and Tulika, Delhi 2003

Dwyer, Rachel – All You Want is Money, All You Need is Love Cassel, New York 2000

Falzon, Mark-Anthony – Paragons of Lifestyle: Gated Communities and the Politics of Space in Bombay City & Society, Berkeley, CA 2004; Vol. 16 Issue 2, pp 145-167

Farrell, Diana and Eric Beinhocker – Next Big Spenders: India's Middle Class McKinsey and Company, 2007

Farrell, Diana and Eric Beinhocker – Tracking the Growth of India's Middle Class McKinsey Quarterly, 2007; No. 3, pp 51-61

Featherstone, Mike – Consumer Culture and Post Modernism Sage Publications, London 1990

Fernandes, Leela – India's New Middle Class: Democratic Politics in an era of Economic Reform University of Minnesota Press, Minneapolis 2006

Fernandes, Leela – Restructuring the New Middle Class in Liberalizing India Comparative Studies of South Asia, Africa and the Middle East, Vo. XX No. 1&2, 2000, pp 88-104

Fishman, Robert – Bourgeois Utopias: The Rise and Fall of Suburbia Basic Books, 1989

Hansen, Thomas Blom – The Saffron Wave Princeton University Press, 1999

Hansen, Thomas Blom – Wages of Violence: Naming and Identity in Post Colonial Bombay

Huyssen, Andreas (ed.) – Other Cities, Other Worlds Duke University Press, 2008

Joshi, Sanjay – Fractured Modernity: Making of a Middle Class in Colonial North India Oxford University Press, New Delhi 2001

King, Anthony – Culture, Globalization and the World System: Contemporary Conditions for the Representation of Identity University of Minnesota Press, 1997

King, Anthony – Spaces of Global Culture: Architecture, Urbanism, Identity Routledge, London 2004

Mawdsley, Emma – India's Middle Class and the Environment Development and Change, 35(1): 2004, pp 7-103

Mazumdar, Ranjani – Bombay Cinema: An Archive of the City University of Minnesota Press, 2007

McKinsey Report – Vision Mumbai: Transforming Mumbai into a World Class City Bombay First, 2003

Miller, Daniel – Material Culture and Mass Consumerism Wiley, 1997

Nijman, Jan – Mumbai's Mysterious Middle Class International Journal of Urban and Regional Research, Vol. 30.4, Dec 2006

Patel, Shirish B – Housing Policies for Mumbai Economic and Political Weekly, August 13 2005, pp 3669-3675

Prakash, Gyan and Kevin Krause (ed.) – The Spaces of the Modern City Princeton University Press, 2008

Princeton University Press, 2001

Rajagopal, Arvind – The Violence of Commodity Aesthetics: Hawkers, Demolition Raids and a New Regime of Consumption Social Text 68, Vol. 19 No. 3, Fall 2001, pp 91-113

Scrase, Tim – The 'New' Middle Class in India: A Re-assessment Conference Paper, Asian Studies Association of Australia, Wollongong, June 2006

Shatkin, Gavin - Planning to forget: informal settlements as 'forgotten places' in globalizing metro Manila Urban Studies, Vol. 41, No. 12, 2469–2484, November 2004, pp 2469-2484

Tiwari, Piyush – House Price Dynamics in Mumbai, 1989-1995 RURDS, Vol. 12 No. 2, July 2000, pp 149-163

The Japanese Apartment: who's public and who's private?

O apartamento japonês: o que é público e o que é privado?

Suma Pandhi

Em sua tese de doutorado Suma Pandhi trabalha a relação entre os espaços públicos e os espaços privados na habitação japonesa, argumentando que existe uma especificidade local na forma de tratar esta transição. Com esse olhar este capítulo se debruça sobre a evolução do apartemento no Japão, mais especificamente na permanência da "engawa" ou espaço de transição.

Beginning in the 1920s, the city of Tōkyō underwent a period of immense change due to modernization and industrialization. During the interwar years of World War I, communication and contact with European goods and culture increased. At the same time, the capital city began to welcome more incomers from other areas in Japan seeking new opportunities. By the 1920s, Tōkyō's population reached three million, a two million-person increase since 1907. In 1923, the Kanto Earthquake changed the urban landscape of Tōkyō greatly.[1] With over 60 percent of the city destroyed due the burning of predominantly timber-constructed buildings, the city faced a period of

---

[1] Roman Cybriswky, Tōkyō (England: John Wiley & Sons Ltd, 1998) 74.

reconstruction.[2] As part of these reconstruction efforts, the Tōkyō Metropolitan Government needed to find a way to handle the middle class housing shortage. The answer arguably changed how public and private space developed in relationship to apartment and city living in modern urban space.

In the 1990s, Toyo Ito developed further postmodern theories relating technology to city, and home life. Subsequently, Tokyo, presents a unique case in comparison to other large cities in Japan and internationally because of its specific phases of construction and reconstruction. As the city has grown and redeveloped, housing has also changed, particularly, the apartment. However, today's Japanese apartment, like many other housing typologies, has its roots in traditional Japanese housing. In order to understand how apartment life and urban lifestyle have developed in Tokyo, an examination of the traditional Japanese floor plan is first necessary, followed by a general analysis of the modern floor plan, and its re-appropriations in projects by Japanese architects SANAA and Riken Yamamoto.

TRADITIONAL JAPANESE FOOR PLAN

The traditional Japanese floor plan is derived from the traditional Japanese home, or minka. These homes were built around the 13th century, using local and affordable materials such as wood, straw, and bamboo.[3] They belong to the non-samurai class in Japan. , making the owners of the minka, middle class owners—such as merchants or farmers. Below is a minka floor plan.

---

[2] Ibid 71.

[3] Yukio. Futagawa. The essential Japanese House; craftsmanship, function and style in Town Country. J Weatherhill: Tokyo, 1967. 36

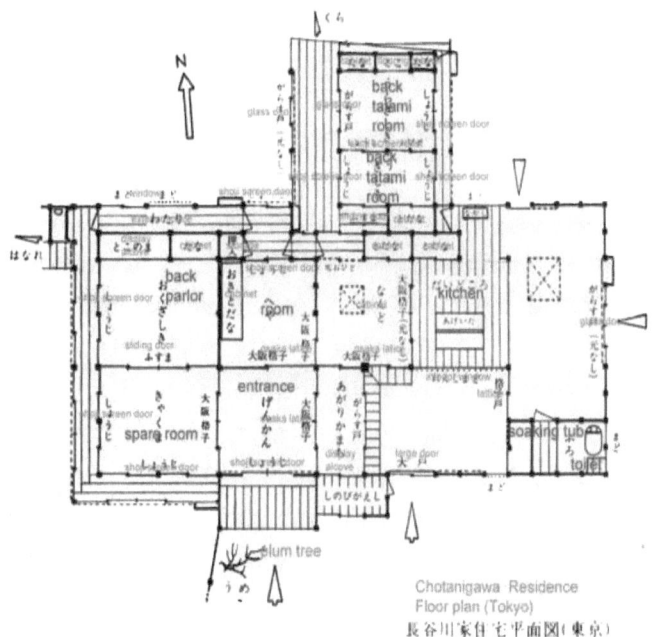

Chotanigawa Residence
Floor plan (Tokyo)
長谷川家住宅平面図（東京）

LIVING AND DINING

In analyzing the floor plan above, three basic areas emerge: living, dining, kitchen. The living areas include the back parlor, back tatami rooms (for sleeping), bathroom area, and rooms. Dining encompasses the area to the left of the kitchen. The bathing area also, comparatively larger than traditional American middle class homes, demonstrates the ritual of bathing in Japanese culture. One washes, and then soaks in the clean water of an ofuro, or hot tub. The kitchen area is close to the genkan but to the side of the home because Japanese cooking was traditionally performed using coal while squatting. [4]

ENTRY AND EXTERIOR SPACES, MOMENTS INBETWEEN

The pronounced entry and exterior space surrounding the residential space blur areas between interior and exterior spaces, are a spatial expression of the Japanese term ma, meaning the spaces in between, or an interval between time and space.[5]The sliding doors, or fusuma, also reflect the ability to change the use of room by opening and closing these doors for more or less space. The fusuma walls allow for relatively little privacy between rooms. Coupled with the measurements of the tatami mat, the traditional Japanese home allows for a greater flexibility of use between rooms. Along with the concept of ma, Shinto beliefs also have influenced the spatialization and choreography of the traditional Japanese home. The genkan, or entry, functions as a threshold between the interior of the home and the natural outside world. When entering a home, the visitor is traditionally received in this space, and must take off his or her shoes and face them towards the entry. This custom, achieved through the space of a genkan, symbolizes a leaving behind of the exterior world.

A display of flowers in the genkan and back parlor also demonstrate moments within the floor plan where one would stop and appreciate the changing flora and painting to reflect a the subsequent change in seasons by the presence of a deciduous tree. This garden was either part of the entry or backside of the house, and was always framed by the sliding shoji or fusuma panels, blurring the visual and physical

---

[4] Jordan Sand, House and Home in Modern Japan: Architecture, Domestic Space, and Bourgeois Culture, 1880-1930 (Cambridge: Harvard University Asia Center, 2003) 196.

5 Nitschke: "Ma-The Japanese Sense of Place

boundaries between exterior and interior spaces. How these spaces begin to translate to the modern apartment, and relate ultimately to the concept of urban space can be perhaps best studied in the Dojunkai Apartments, a prototype for modernist apartments.

AOYAMA DOJUNKAI APARTMENTS

In 1924, the Dojunkai Association was officially established through the Tōkyō Metropolitan Government to address the need for new housing following the Kanto Earthquake of 1923 that caused the destruction of timber housing in the city. The association was headed by Uchida Shozo, who had also been an active member of the Kenchiku Gakkai, an association that conducted various studies on housing reform and planning in Tōkyō. Uchida was quite informed by the cultural exchange and dialogue regarding modernist European housing, particularly Germany, at the time. At the same time, the Dojunkai association performed a variety of tests on concrete as an earthquake proof construction material for the new apartments.[6] This testing was innovative in Japan at the time. Furthermore, Le Corbusier and Gropius, modernists who valued form as an expression of function, influenced the architecture of these housing complexes. This design value was thoroughly reflected in the design and layout of the Dojunkai Apartments. [7]

However, this European modernist architecture was also appropriated to the Japanese lifestyle and the context of the home (i.e. sentō,

---

[6] Marco Pompilli. Dojunkai Apartments 1924- 1934. 39. Pompilli also notes the proposed site plans of the Tōkyō Government by German architects Ende and Beckmann in 1887.

[7] Uchida Collection. "Aoyama Apartment House Concrete Testing", (Tōkyō Metropolitan Archives, 1924).

public bathing areas, and tatami rooms). In addition to this, the Garden City Movement, a city planning movement taking root in the U.S and Europe that encouraged a greater human interaction with natural surroundings, influenced the planning of the site. In total, the Dojunkai Tōkyō that were highly innovative and influential.

FLOOR PLAN

Below is the floor plan of the Aoyama Dojunkai Apartments. According to Pompilli, the Dojunkai floor plans were developed through the rotation of the cell rooms to enable exterior and interior circulation without a clear visual hierarchy, Pompilli states:

 In the Japanese language, and therefore Japanese society, a person is conceived as a flexible and easily connectable individual, as part of a much larger whole, from which the person is separate and yet to which it belongs...The abstract model of the Dojunkaiapartment minimal housing complex suggests a reflection on the category of the whole on the factors that organize it as such. Within the Dojunkai type organizational structure, we therefore recognize a building unit consisting of a rigid skin and a flexible skeleton... The minimal housing complex system is organized by means of a de-composition, with components re-assembled according to a system of autonomous andcontinuous layers: the linear layer of the housing units...the street's network layer, and the green public layer. (Pompilli 145)

As shown in the floor plan above, sliding shoji doors surround most of the rooms, creating a grid like system within the home. Through opening, closing, and even changing the location of these doors consistent with a grid system, the ideal of modularity emerges within the tradition of the Japanese home that Pompilli proposes. Therefore, this concept of modularity was not new to the residential spaces, however, the structural system of reinforced concrete, was a material new to Japan.

As Pompilli discusses, the modularity of the floor plan results in a layering of floor plan within semipublic and public spaces consistent with influential urban planning theories at the time. This layering of scale in terms of the public urban space, and private residential space through modularity are reappropriations of the traditional Japanese home through the home, and surrounding garden. The floor plan above below, however, is transparently labeled. The bathroom, kitchen, stairway areas, and tatami rooms are not clearly defined. This openness happens subsequently at two scales: within the residential floor plan and the larger apartment building itself as shown below.

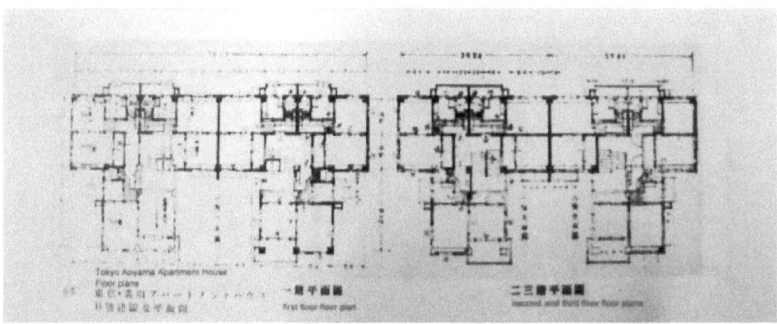

This new typology, a construct of traditional Japanese housing within the trajectory of modernism, was transformative in Japanese collective housing, and can be seen most strongly in the development of the mansion or LDK housing typology.

THE EMERGENCE OF THE LDK

While there are a large number of apartment projects by well-known architects in Japan, the floor plans below are examples of a typical Mansion apartment. This history of mansion apartments is not been widely studied yet, as is the name change from apartment to mansion following the Dojunkai Apartments.[8] Similar to tatami mats in minka housing, tatami mats are used in apartments as a standard of measurement (33"x 70.5"). Here, the overall floor typology remains the same: entrance, soaking tub for bathing, and tatami rooms. However, balcony becomes an extension of the blurring of boundaries between the interior and exterior spaces.

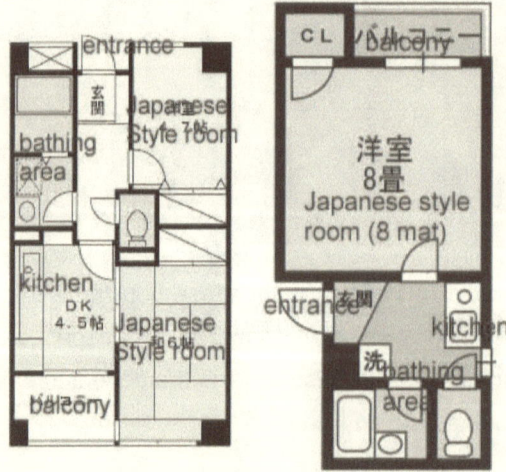

1DLK   2DLK

---

[8] http://www.geocities.jp/tshny046/rekisi.html

Examined closely, the Dojunkai became a transformative typology for collective housing that was then translated into the idea of the mansion, whose parcel was smaller in scale as the city grew after WWII. However as Tokyo moved past her post war state and into a technology driven world with the Bubble economy, the idea of the endless city in Japan began to take on larger implications within collective housing. The following case studies will examine this translation from traditional Japanese home into the postmodern urban Japanese dweller.

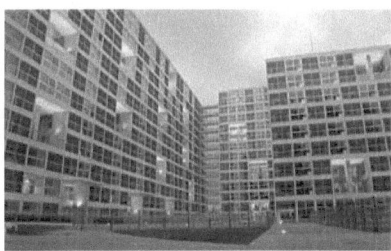 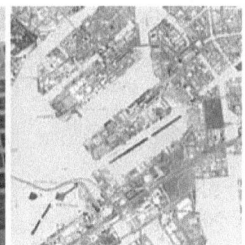

SHINONOME CANAL COURT

In 2003, along with a group of other well-known Japanese architects, such as Kengo Kuma and, Riken Yamamoto co designed a block of apartments in Tokyo with Toyo Ito. He describes the project:

The main characteristics of this housing development are the common terrace' which is a volume carved out of the residential building, the 'foyer-room' which can be used as a home office, sunny center corridors, and sunny bathrooms. Placed randomly on each floor, a common terrace of double height is surrounded with foyer-rooms. Connected to common terraces, people can use these foyer rooms as SOHO, nursery space, or hobby rooms. Each common terrace is surrounded by the 'foyer rooms' of eighthousing units. One fourth of the units face the common terraces. The other units are separated from the center corridors with glass partitions. Because of the terraces that occur at intervals through out the project, these center corridors have the light and aircirculation of an exterior space. Placing the foyer rooms by the center corridors can make the residential rooms open toward the corridor. To allow for large, square foyer rooms, bathrooms, and kitchens are by the outer wall. This blend of homes and workplaces rather than home next to workplace. We tried to enlarge the potential of collective housing, putting function of office into housing[9]

By mixing the exterior space with the interior, more private aspects of the program, Yamamoto is working within the construct of the Japanese traditional home and the Dojunkai. As shown in the diagram below, Yamamoto has re-arranged the entrance into the apartment unit by treating the corridor (6') as a public threshold, but at the same time maintained a layering of public and private spaces in relationship to the primary entrance of the house. [10]

As a result, the public corridor begins to function more like the engawa, or threshold of the Japanese home and the garden space are re-appropriated into F rooms or Terraces-work place or public spaces, respectively. As Yamamoto has noted, home and work are now blending in Japan—so the garden, while still public in nature, is now used programmatically as a work place or meeting place, public uses, for the postmodern urban dweller.

Therefore, the spatial layout of the home maintains its traces of the traditional Japanese home over 700 years ago. At the same time, however, it can be argued that the modularity and open space of the Dojunkai apartments are reflected in Yamamoto's floor plans.

---

[9] www. rikenyamamoto.co.jp

[10] Hilary French. New Urban Housing. Lawrence King Publishing: 2006, 139.

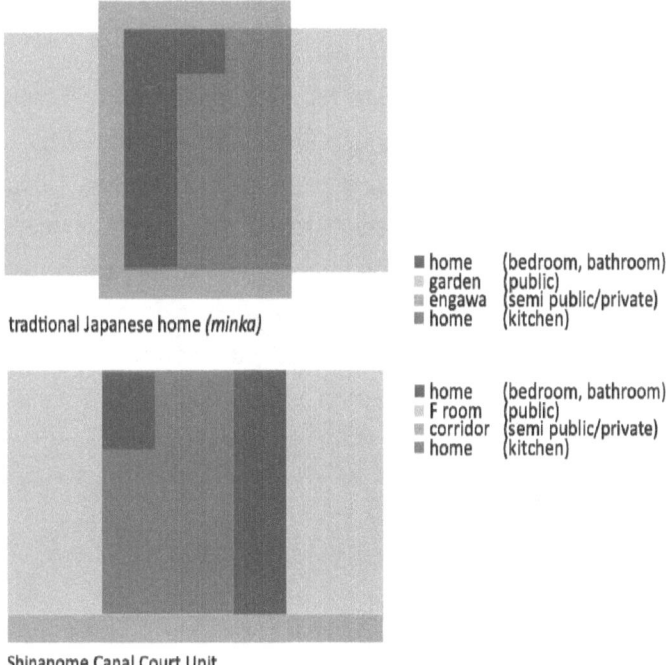

tradtional Japanese home *(minka)*

■ home (bedroom, bathroom)
garden (public)
■ engawa (semi public/private)
■ home (kitchen)

■ home (bedroom, bathroom)
F room (public)
corridor (semi public/private)
■ home (kitchen)

Shinanome Canal Court Unit

Within the flow of the open space from one room to the next, Yamamoto's plan also suggests a pixelization of public and private activities. Though private and public spaces are adjacent to each other, there are moments where semi public program (kitchen) and private program (bathroom) are suddenly interacting with on another. In many ways, the Shinanome Canal Court project suggests a hybrid of modern Japan and pre modern concepts of space that are based on Japanese responses and re appropriations of modernism and part of a continued construct of traditional Japanese space.

GIFU KITAGATA APARTMENTS

Built in 2001, the Gifu Kitagata apartments (Sejima wing) were designed by the Japanese firm SANAA, headed by Kazuyo Sejima and Ryue Nishizawa. Consisting of kitchen, bedroom, dining, common room, and tatami room, the project employs a modularity consistent with Dojunkai principles of space. Each room is the same size (8. 5 ft x15.5 ft).[11] ON the south side of the project, there is a verandah that allows for access into each room of the space. On the North side of the project is the corridor. With an public and semi

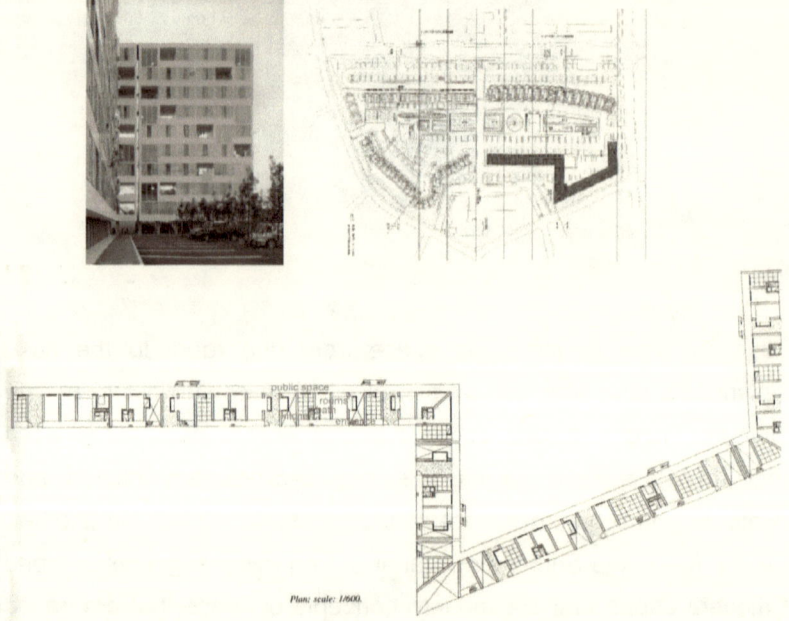

Plans scale: 1/600.

public pathway that surrounds the five rooms, that in turn in case the most private spaces of the program of bedroom and bathroom by kitchen, terrace and living room, the project takes on the traditional Japanese home in a postmodern condition. The engawa is now the

---

[11] Hilary French. 180.

terrace, corridor, and verandah. The most private parts of the program are all still located towards the center of the home.

In comparison to Shinanome Project, the Kitagata apartments rely on the engawa as a major part of circulation within public, semi public, and private parts of the home. With out this main artery that surrounds the home, consistent with the engawa and garden of the Japanese home, movement between exterior and interior spaces are not possible. As with the traditional Japanese home, the garden in this project is the spatial re-appropriation of the terrace. Private space becomes public and public space becomes private.

FURTHER READINGS

The two case studies presented in this paper are part of an emerging typology of Japanese collective housing that has begun to develop in Japan today. Firms such as Cat headed by Kojima Kazuhiro and Akamatsu Kazumi, Sou Fujimoto, and others are beginning to suggest further nuanced ideas of the Japanese home within the larger urban context of the Japanese apartment home. In their project Nozawa Apartment Block, CAt explores various blocks of space that tenant can chose in a Tokyo neighborhood. As shown in their diagrammed cube below and example floor plan, they are arguably deconstructing the most private spaces of the Japanese home and exploding them across open spaces. The layout still exists, but walls and relationship to public access- though one main stairway is moved to the center of the building; opposite from the then previous projects.

However, the staircase core still functions similarly to the engawa, a threshold, and movement between exterior and interior spaces that are now both public and private, or as Yamamoto, would say, all private. These changes are related to the scale of the city and affordability of parcel unit.   As the Japanese urban landscape continues to grow and condense at the same time, collective housing will become part of a larger discussion of constructs of traditional domestic space as well as new appropriations and new spatial typologies of the Japanese home in the city that suggested further nuanced or a disappearance of readings of public and private space.

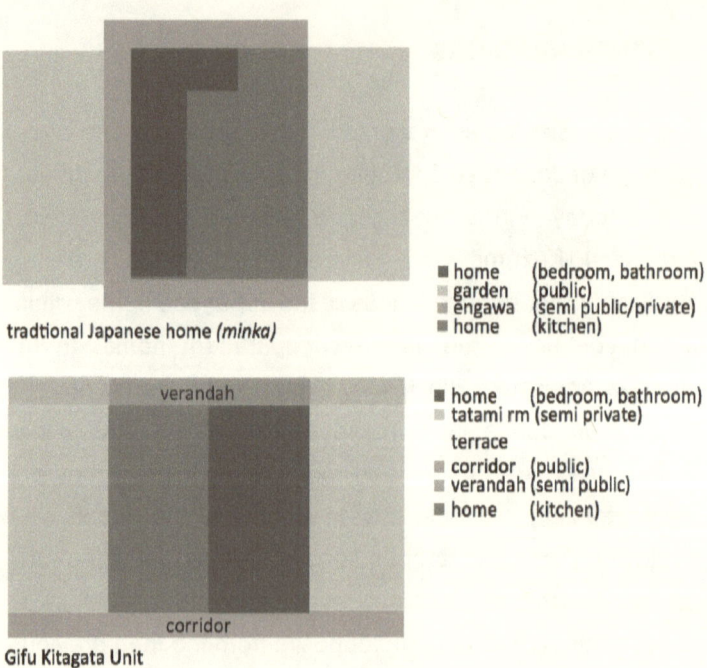

tradtional Japanese home *(minka)*

■ home   (bedroom, bathroom)
▨ garden   (public)
▨ engawa   (semi public/private)
■ home   (kitchen)

verandah

■ home   (bedroom, bathroom)
▨ tatami rm (semi private)
  terrace
▨ corridor (public)
▨ verandah (semi public)
■ home   (kitchen)

corridor

Gifu Kitagata Unit

REFERENCES

Baba, Yasuhiro. Design of the Dojunkai. Ed. United Design Inc.Tōkyō:
Matsushiki Co Architectural Research Materials, 2000.

Bourdier, Marc. Dojunkai apato no genkei: Nihon no kechikushi ni okeru
yakuwari (Dojunkai housing prototypes : the role played in the Japanese
history of architecture). Tōkyō, 1992.

Cybriwsky, Roman .Tōkyō, the changing profile of an urban giant. London :
Belhaven Press, 1991.

French, Hilary. New Urban Housing. Laurence King Publishing, 2006.

Fujimori, T. Meiji no Tōkyō keikaku. (Plan for Meiji Tōkyō). Tōkyō: Iwanami
Shoten, 1982.

Futugawa, Yukio. The essential Japanese house; craftmanship, function, and
style in town and country. Text and commentaries: Teiji Itoh. Tokyo, J.
Weatherhill, [1967]

Hidenobu. Jinnai. Translated by Kimiko Nishimura.Tōkyō A Spatial
Anthropology. Berkley: University of California Press, 1995.

Hur, Nam-lin. Prayer and Play in Late Tokugawa Japan: Asakusa Sensÿji and
Edo Society. Harvard East Asian Monograph. Cambridge MA: Harvard UP,
2001.

Interview with Riken Yamomoto, June 8, 2008. www.riken-yamamoto.co.jp

Ōnishi Hiroshi, Umeda Sadahiro. "Dai Tōkyō" kūkan no seijishi: 1920-30-
nendai (Great Tōkyō: Politics of Space during 1920-1930.)

Pompili. Marco. Dojunkai Apartments : Tōkyō 1924-1934 : l'abitazione
collettiva giapponese e la città moderna = collective housing in Japan and the
modern city. Roma : Librerie Dedalo, c2001.

Sand, Jordan. House and Home in Modern Japan: Architecture, Domestic
Space, and Bourgeois Culture, 1880-1930.Cambridge: Harvard University
Asia Center, 2003.

Seidensticker. Edward. Low city, high city : Tōkyō from Edo to the
earthquake. New York : Knopf, 1983.

Uchida Archive Collection. Kenchiku Shyashinruishu Shinkou Apatomento
1927 Tōkyō Metropolitan Archives.

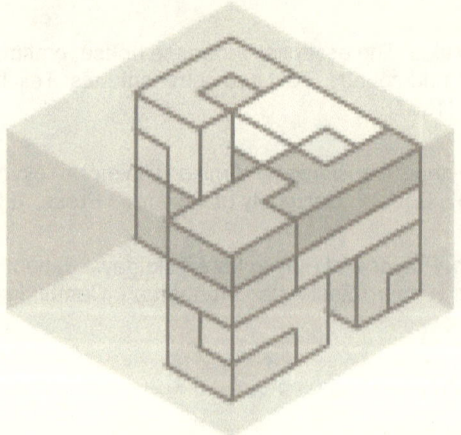

SPACE BLOCK NOZAWA

Living similarly in different apartments: Moscow

Vidas iguais em apartamentos diferentes: Moscow

Vera Baranova

A evolução da moradia na Russia, da tradicional IZBA aos apartamentos Stalinistas é única dado o vigor da experimentação das vanguardas e a rapidez das transformações. Mas enquanto muito já se escreveu sobre as vanguardas russas, pouco se sabe do viver contemporâneo em Moscou, foco da pesquisa do Global Apartments Researcg Group. Dos questionarios trabalhados por Vera Baranova em 2006/2007 foram várias as surpresas. Em primeiro lugar é sabido que o custo da habitação em Moscou figura entre os mais caros do mundo mas quando dividido pelo salário médio da Russia (U\$ 839 por mês) perceb-se o tamanho do problema. Enquanto a Russia acompanha os demais países Europeus com taxas de fertilidade baixíssimas e uma população envelhecendo rapidamente, os questionários mostraram uma média superior a 4 habitantes por unidade o que é muito alto e reflexo do custo proibitivo da moradia. Tendo um apartamento de 2 quartos em torno de 45m2, a área disponível por habitante fica perto de 10m2, bem abaixo dos 12m2 defendidos pelo CIAM no início do século e perto dos 9m2 encontrados em nossas pesquisas nas favelas brasileiras.

The housing solution for the 21st century Moscow apartment does not differ much from the rest of the contemporary urban centers around the globe, being populated by thousands of high-rise buildings. Russia's housing evolution from the vernacular izba (traditional Russian countryside dwelling) to the modern apartment block and the contemporary 21st century apartment is quite unique in its comparison to other urban center developments in the rest of the world. The Global Apartments Research Group has been exploring various characteristics of typical housing solutions, including apartment layout, size and its development over the last few hundred years. Evaluating the data, we can understand how a typical modernist housing approach is adopted to the Russian lifestyle. The questionnaires sent out to several households in Moscow allow for an investigation on the issue of domesticity and spatial utilization within those apartments. The surge in the construction of the new upscale high rise apartment towers is quite a jump from the quite ordinary Stalinist apartment blocks of the 20th century. This new development in the housing sector suggests the changes that are now occurring within the urban center and possibly the changes the way a typical Russian family may now live.

Just like in São Paulo, Seoul, Mumbai, Tokyo along with many city centers of the world, the high rise buildings are overtaking the skyline of those fast growing metropolises. In the last decade Moscow has experienced a large population growth. People come from abroad as well as rural areas of Russia, all in search of work opportunity, as it has been the case in many other cities where people come to better their lives in search of better jobs and higher quality of life. The housing market in Moscow has become a big social demand. The apartments are not only needed for the new residents of the city, but also for those who are fortunate to relocate to another apartment.

In the Soviet times, the government policy of providing mandatory housing for every citizen and their family was rapidly growing. As the population of Moscow increased, this led to many construction projects around the city. This resulted in typical housing blocks which were largely prefabricated and replicated throughout not only Moscow, but many other cities in Russia as well. The housing blocks can be differentiated by "style" according to the neighborhoods they were in and which materials they were used to built them. These housing blocks received a name after the leader who was in power during the time when the building was built. Leninists apartments, Stalinists apartments, Khrushchev apartments. Private ownership of apartments people were living in was limited to select few. Only after the fall of the Soviet Union, people secured the rights to own the places in which they were living. When social housing projects started to be built in Moscow, back in the beginning of the 20th century, they formed the face of the city, the environment that now can be found almost anywhere in its the metropolitan area. The majority of current Moscow population lives in Stalinist and Khrushchev era housing.

Since the dissolution of USSR, market economy emerged in Moscow. The market economy allowed many aspects in Muscovite culture to westernize and globalize. But the cost of living in a new high rise in the outskirts is just as expensive as living downtown in a Stalinist era building. Due to such a high demand in housing in the last decade, the prices of the apartments have been rising at a higher rate than ever. The city developers, certain government official and the investors are making a lot of money from such economic demand in the housing industry.[1] Depending on the neighborhood, one could pay average of $7000 per square meter (11 square feet) in downtown Moscow and an average of $4000 per square meter in the outer regions.[2] It would cost one to pay about $2500 a month for a one bedroom apartment and about $1500 a month for a studio, if both are located in the downtown neighborhoods.[3] These prices seem normal for North American and / or European centers but we should remember that the average monthly wage in Moscow is below US$ 900.00. Given the numbers, it becomes impossible for a single average person to afford even a studio in downtown. Besides, given the demand, it has been projected that the newly constructed apartment (for example the "Golden Island" development) can rise to a price of $30,000 per square meter.4 (For realty costs in 2006, see image 1).

As far as the sizes of those apartments, a typical one bedroom apartment is about thirty square meters (323 square feet), a typical two bedroom apartment is forty five square meters (485 square feet), and a typical three bedroom apartment is seventy square meters (753 square feet). With such a tight living space, families get accustomed to a close relationship with each other. In our questionnaire sample the average household size was 4.5 (very high for contemporary European households) which would give some families as little as 110 sqft (10 sqm) per person. A constant invasion of space becomes so natural that one does not become conscious of such a fact. This is why privacy becomes a luxury, and thus apartments with larger living areas become harder to afford.

For many decades in the 20th century one single apartment (usually a two/three rooms) would house the entire family, typically a family consisting of two parents, a child or two, and a grandparent. As the children were growing up and getting married, the opportunities to own their own places were not presented as they could not be afforded, so they stayed at the apartment that were privatized by their parents or grandparents. Only a small percentage of the population, and usually those in the upper classes, could afford to own a new apartment, and they usually choose those that are being built in the outskirts of the city.

As been happening the last few years, select families were fortunate enough to be relocated from older Stalinist buildings into newly constructed ones. Open areas for new developments are hard to find in Moscow. Building farther away from the city center creates a longer commute, which becomes highly undesirable for those who have to travel far for work or school. A new policy has been established to take down older buildings built in mid 20th century, and relocate families who were living in those apartments to the newly constructed ones nearby. Those older buildings were taken down to make room for new ones to be built in the upcoming years.

The Global Apartments Research Group has been conducting research and working together to collect data on apartments, housing costs, living environment to try to understand the conditions of living in not only the new high rises, but also in the mid 20th century apartment block. In the research, collecting and drawing plans of apartments of different eras, different sizes and different layouts aids us in understanding social and cultural impact of the high rise, this only recently developed housing phenomenon. We learned that certain areas of an apartment are more public while others are more private. In westernized culture it has been custom to treat living spaces as public while keeping bedrooms as private. For hundreds of years in Russia, communal living has established a cultural trait. It has been encouraged since the first izba was built (when it first appeared is not precisely known, but the first introduction has been traced to 500 A.D.),5 where public and private spaces were shared.

Back in those days, the kitchen was considered more sacred – a woman's space, while living space was where the husband would gather with his friends. Today, in a Russian apartment, a kitchen is still considered woman's space; however it also becomes a gathering space. A kitchen today is a space for cooking, dining, and bringing the family together after a long day of work. The bedrooms and the living spaces are almost indistinguishable, based on how much room one has in their apartment and how many people are living there.

When one goes to buy or rent an apartment, the advertisement would generally read something to an effect of "two room apartment for sale/rent". The apartment with two rooms (including kitchen, bathroom, and water closet room) would not necessarily differentiate between the uses of these rooms, which is different from the way a similar apartment in United States would be advertized – "two bedroom apartment" for example. Unless the apartment is fully furnished and planned out by an architect or an interior designer, the rooms would not clearly indicate living or bedroom spaces. The family would choose how to navigate, inhabit, and live in their own apartment. Although privacy is desired, it is not always achieved. A young couple might sleep in one bedroom, while have a couch with a television (a gathering space) in another room, and have that room be where one of their grandparents sleeps at night as well. It could also be that the family has a little kid who would sleep in one of the rooms, either with his parents or the grandparent. The grandparent would take the kid to the kindergarten during the day while parents are at work, while themselves spending the entire day in the kitchen preparing dinner.

The questionnaire element of the research allowed us to more confidently understand such issue. We asked people taking the questionnaire to draw their apartment to the best of their ability and to annotate which room they spend their time in every fifteen minutes during a full typical day. What we found out was that usually a person would sleep, study and entertain in one common room. It is typical for a person to sleep in the same room, which would technically call it their own room. However it would also be common to entertain and bring guests to the same room. These rooms become public at one time of day, while private at another time.

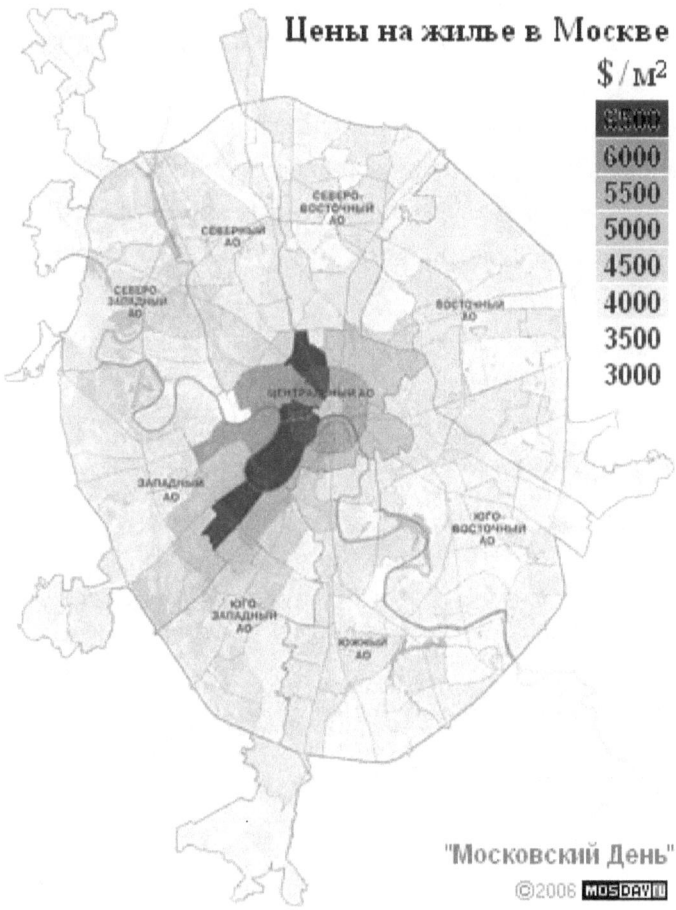

Real Estate Prices for Moscow in 2006 (prices are listed in $/per square meter)

The Moscow housing scene is developing rapidly. The westernization that has been occurring in the country drives the desire of the capital's inhabitants to change their home lifestyle. It challenges the developers to build a larger number of apartments, providing more room and privacy for the families that would be living there in the future. It challenges the young generation to find their own niche at home, while those who are granted the privilege of privacy will begin to establish a new social culture that Moscow has rarely seen. Families have been getting their opportunities to better their living, being relocated to newer developments at no cost. This becomes much harder for the elderly who got very much accustomed to living in their apartment for decades, the apartment that has been granted to them by the state. Just having property rights to their apartment is already a luxury in their eyes.

---

1 Humphries, Connor. *Dividing the Spoils of the Boom.* The Moscow Times, http://www.stroi.ru/eng/default.aspx?d =5&dr=901&m=13

2 Information Agency Regnum. *Absolute Record of Realty Cost is Broken,* http://www.regnum.ru/news/643249.html

3Humphries, Connor. *Dividing the Spoils of the Boom.* The Moscow Times, http://www.stroi.ru/eng/default.aspx?d =5&dr=901&m=13

4 Information Agency Regnum. *Absolute Record of Realty Cost is Broken,* http://www.regnum.ru/news/643249. html

5 Hellie, Richard. (2001). "The Russian Smoky Hut and Its Probable Health Consequences." *Russian History* 28(1 - 4):171 - 184.

The Emergence of the Apartment Building in Egypt

As origens do edifício de apartamentos no Egito

Omar Baghdady

Os leitores brasileiros com certeza se lembram de Hassan Fathy quandos e fala em arquitetura Egipcia. Mas se as estruturas de barro ficaram marcadas na memória dos arquitetos pelo mundo a fora, elas estão longe de representar o que se fez no Egito ao longo do século XX. Omar Baghdady está terminando sua tese de doutorado sobre a Arquitetura Moderna no Egito em particular sobre a obra de Sayyid Kurayim. O capítulo que se segue é a parte da tese que trata da evolução do edifício de apartamentos no Cairo.

One of the earliest comprehensive studies on the apartment building as a building type was published in al-'imara architectural journal in 1957. A series of articles written by Tawfik 'Abdel-Gawad, a prominent architectural scholar, under the title, "The Modern Flat" (al-'imara al-sakaniya) presented its attributes, formal characteristics, and social benefits. It was considered a novel building type, one that was crucial for modern Egyptian society. In his opening paragraph he alludes to this importance:

Due to the importance of the role played by modern flats in shaping the economy and the development and sustenance of the city, I found it my duty as an architect with a message and with a responsibility towards my society and nation to study this topic and publish it in a series of articles in this journal.

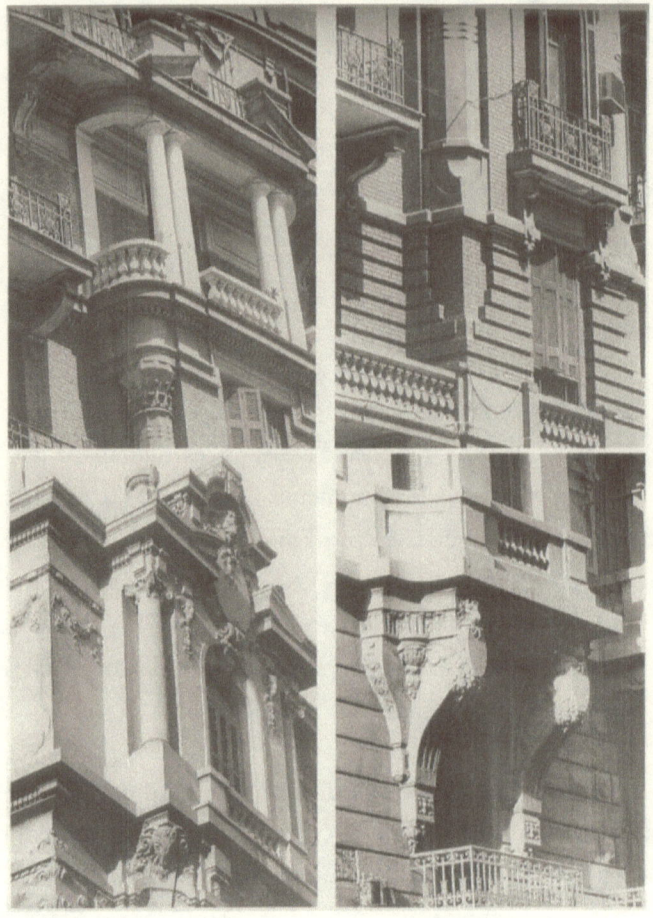

Figure 1, Different Architectural styles in Cairo between the late 19th century and early 20th. (Reference: Mohamed Scharabi 1987)

The series of articles come after two decades of fascination with the building type by Egyptian architects and the editors of al-`Imara Journal. The journal gave great attention to the discussion of apartment buildings as a fundamental type in Egypt's built environment. In the twenty years that the journal was published there were approximately 30 apartment house projects illustrated and 7 essays that discussed the type in terms of standards, design criteria, construction methods, social implications and spatial considerations. Collectively, this body of literature constituted one of the main sources on apartment buildings in Egypt at the time.

HISTORY OF TYPE

Throughout the early twentieth century the apartment house grew to be the main form of residence for the Egyptians. Neither local precedents to the apartment house, nor any prescribed formula from abroad could appropriately fulfill the needs of a new social structure that was taking form in Egypt by the 1930s. This new social reality was driven by changes in family structure, economic development, and political advances. Whereas the extended family may have been dominant in the late nineteenth century, by the 1930's this phenomenon had receded greatly. and the nuclear family became more prominent. Similarly women became more accepted by society. They could now gain education, had civil rights, and participated in public discourse.

Concurrently, the growth of an Egyptian middle class to increased education, welfare and modernization required a new housing form that would accommodate their needs.[1] Due to these changes, apartment buildings appeared to be the most appropriate model since they allowed greater family independence, offered the growing middle class chances to invest, presented a modern image that was aspired to by the different classes, and at the same time, its spatial configuration allowed a degree of flexibility to accommodate changing

---

[1] For more details on the emergence of the middle class in Egypt refer to Luis `Awad, Nash'at al-Aristocratia al-Misria, *Tarikh al-fikr al-massri al-hadith*. Vol.1 section 1, 307-336. Cairo: al-hay'a al-`amma lil kitab. and Clariss L. Pollard, Nurturing the Nation: The Family Politics of the 1919 Egyptian Revolution, Ph.D, Department of History, University of California, Berkely, 1997.

needs. Since the precedents in Cairo primarily served the upper classes or the European nationals. The new circumstances required a re-definition of the type. The history of apartment buildings in Egypt remains, however, ambiguous. The complexity of the type shed light onto the development of modern society in Egypt in this very critical period in modern history.

Most of the scholarship on apartment buildings attributes its origins to the Parisian model of the mid 1800s due to the growth of a French bourgeoisie.[2] As for Egypt, the French model is simply one of many residential typologies that influenced the type as it took shape in Egypt. The 20th century apartment building in Egypt had varied spatial configurations. These configurations and characteristics differed according to socio-cultural factors such as wealth, class, and education, as well as context, plot size, building codes and zoning laws. At the same time earlier residential typologies provided key spatial patterns that influenced the formal and spatial organizations of the new type. All these factors together gave it a degree of complexity and appeal that distinguished it from other typologies.

The new apartment house represented a shift from earlier architectural articulations of space. They represented a curious relationship between public and private. On one hand, apartment units were quite autonomous and thus, provided a high level spatial privacy. On the other hand, the increased size of the buildings, and their incorporation of vestibules, lobbies and elaborate stairways, meant that they allowed more public interaction in these "undesignated" spaces. For Egyptians to accept such spatial relations

---

[2] Sharon Marcus, *Apartment Stories: City and Home in nineteenth-century Paris and London* (Berkeley: University of California Press, 1999), 19-32. Refer also to Michael Dennis, *Court and Garden: From the French Hôtel to the City of Modern Architecture*, (Cambridge: MIT Press, 1986).

by the early twentieth century, this meant that an evolution from the traditional Arab-Ottoman house which was common throughout the urban centers must have taken place in the second half of the 19th century.

Evidence of the origins of this change can be associated with the emergence of the "Rumi style" in the mid nineteenth century and its continued use until the close of the century. This style was presented as a mixture of European and Arabic-Ottoman architectures and was commented on by Clot Bey, Mohamed Ali's physician, in his celebrated work on Egyptian architecture as "the bastard genre, a fusion of the bad taste of the Greek [classical] style degenerated with the Arab style."[3] By comparing the facades of a typical Cairene Arabic-Ottoman and a Rumi house we notice a shift in the formal laws. These formal transformations are not just aesthetic variations; they presented more subtle cultural ones. From the elimination of mashrabiyas (wooden arabesques) with their associated cultural implications and replacing them with a more abstract European shutter windows; to the introduction of balconies and, more importantly, the disappearance of the open courtyard and the introduction of the central hall or sala. These transformations can be understood as stylistic changes and alterations due to the interactions between cultures and the dominance of one over the other.[4] They, however, must be examined in terms of cultural transformations in society, which adopted such forms in order to manifest these changes.

---

[3] Nihal Tamarz, *Nineteenth-century Cairene houses and palaces* (Cairo: American University in Cairo Press, 1998), 24.

[4] Nihal Tamarz, 25

Over time these formal impositions became more acceptable by society. For example, Mohamed Ali banned mashrabiyas on facades and ordered the removal of mastabas (brick benches) from the streets to facilitate the flow of traffic. His most drastic urban intervention was to tear down the gates to the harat (alleys).[5] Moreover, a Ministry of Public Works was established, Majlis Tanzim Misr al-Mahrousa (1847), to manage the process of naming the streets and numbering the buildings. These interventions and establishments caused crucial changes to the urban culture of Cairo establishing new sensibilities of public and private as functionally distinct realms in opposition to the more fluid relationships that existed earlier.

Nevertheless, these spatial and formal changes soon began to reflect shifts in Egyptian culture such as gender relations and accessibility to public space, while maintaining those aspects of the local culture that were fundamental and adapting the foreign influence to comply.

THE EUROPEAN MODEL

In 1967 Khedive Ismail, grandson of Mohamed Ali visited Paris to attend the Exposition Universalle which represented Baron Haussmann's piece de resistance. Haussmann showed the Khedive the different projects that were implemented in modern Paris such as Champs de Mars and the gardens of Bois de Boulogne . The impact of Haussmann's vision of the modern city was enormous on the Khedive. Aiming to associate Egypt with the "civilized" nations, he aimed to transform Cairo. Under the supervision of Ali Mubarak, the Minister of Public Works, the designs for the new quarters, namely,

---

[5] Tamarz 1998, 5.

the Isma'ilia quarters, were executed.[6] According to Abu-Lughod, the plots were given out free of cost to wealthy merchants and princes who built villas with surrounding gardens.[7] The new building type, the European apartment house was introduced in this period and flourished after the British occupation in 1882.[8] Primarily used by the foreigners located in the new neighborhood, the apartment houses manifested the new urban culture. However, as mentioned above, the Cairene's were not necessarily astonished by this building type and did not find them contradicting with their own values. The emergence of Egyptian technocrats in the first decades of the 20th century, in addition to the earlier developments of the Rumi house mentioned earlier naturally led to the adoption of the apartment house as the primary urban housing type by the 1910's.

By the 1940's the apartment house was being re-defined as a modern housing type. Abdel-Gawad defined the type according to three different groups: the owners, the tenants, and the architects. For the owners the apartment house was basically a financial investment aiming maximum profitability. As for the tenants, it was their living space,

"the home that shelter's [them]; it is a means of satisfying [their] personal, residential and social needs and also provides comfort, and safety." [9] For the architects it was a creative task aiming to provide the other groups with their needs in the most appropriate manner.

---

[6] Janet Abu-Lughod, *Cairo: 1001 years of the City Victorious* (Princeton, N.J.: Princeton University Press, 1971), 81.

[7] Abu-Lughod 1971, 81.

[8] For more details about the building activities in the time refer to Roger Owen, The Cairo Buidling Industry and the Building Boom of 1887 to 1907.Paper read at Colloque Internationale sur L'histoire du Caire, 1969.

[9] Abdel-Gawad, 1957, 32

As such, it was the architect's responsibility to design the efficient residence. A good design was one that followed "correct scientific rules" in order to fulfill the required functions (wazifa), and needs based on the desires of the different user groups. To elaborate his point further, the complexity of the mechanical systems, plumbing, heating, electrical systems, gas, and fenestration were explained in analogy to the human physiological systems. In his argument, the apartment house was the essential modern residence for the new society.

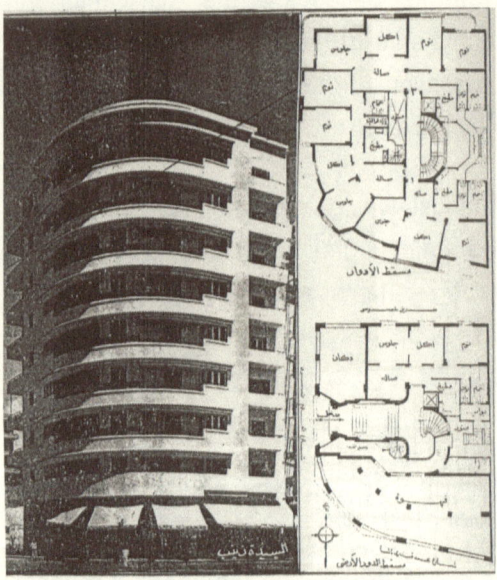

Figure 2. Apartment house in Saida Zeinab neighborhood. the basic organization of the house is not very different from other middle class houses. This simply represents a more humble design in terms of size and spaciousness. (Refernce: Salama 1951)

On dealing with the apartment house, Egyptian architects presented a new attitude towards local cultural norms such as class structure, and social hierarchy. Themes of functionality, efficiency, and social good that they regularly promoted were used to support these inherited social norms. In their efforts to widen their clientele and promote their practice, the architects began to work for other social groups but maintained a class distinction that preserved them from being mistaken with common builders. In an article by `Ali Gabr in 1941, regarding an apartment house in the popular (sha`bia) neighborhood of al-Saida Zeinab, he developed a model for the criteria that should be considered when designing for popular quarters. He divided the considerations into 7 points: the class (tabaqa) that resides the neighborhood, the financial affordability of that class, the spatial needs and requirements, number of rooms, room dimensions and auxiliary spaces, the spatial configuration of the apartments, and finally, economy in terms of the building techniques and choice of materials without compromising beauty and use.[10]

This class consciousness was very important and clearly supported their roles as taste professionals. More interestingly, Gabr's reservations about the popular areas in the essay were limited to the bad spatial solutions, ugliness of the buildings, and harmful economizing that persisted. He did not comment on the culture of these groups or claim a necessity to change their ways and make them more modern. He accepted the difference, worked within its norms and simply, tried to enhance and refine it. Up until the late 50's his model was apparently the most influential. In an article in 1957 by `Abdel-Gawad, the same points were mentioned with very little modification.[11] To what extent these architects actually reflected the needs of the lower income groups still needs to be studied.

Class was not only influential on such abstract levels as shown above. Different classes meant different social backgrounds. These

---

[10] Ali Labib Gabr,`imarat al-'ahya' al-wataniya. *Majalit al-`imara*, no. 2 (1941): 65

[11] `Abdel-Gawad 1957, 31

differences were respected and incorporated in the designs. "Style" (tiraz) [12] was an integral part of representing class discrepancies and as a result the architects were caught between being seen as modern while catering to acceptable social norms. As such, styles were not explicitly discussed in any project descriptions although they definitely existed in the designs through the forms and organizational schemes. It was not presented as an aesthetic code as earlier perceptions of style might have entailed, rather as personal taste and preference.[13] The apartment house of `Ali Labib Gabr in Zamalik showed this integration of Modernist exterior forms and interior, stylized ones. Al-`imara dedicated various articles to the discussion of the notion of style and stylistic architecture. These concepts will be dealt with in more detail later in the paper.

This relation between class and style subsisted from earlier decades. Presenting the house as an exhibit of class, wealth and sophistication of culture had become an integral part of Egyptian society since the late 1900's. Al-Hilal al-Mussawir magazine, which had been active in Egypt since 1882, regularly published photographs of houses of public figures such as Sa`ad Zaghloul and Hoda Sha`rawy highlighting their taste in furniture, décor, arrangements, and valuable antique collections. Moreover, in a detailed monograph on Egypt, Twentieth Century Impressions of Egypt (1909), the Egyptian upper class was represented through interiors of the receptions, studies and

---

[12] Style here is regarded as specific classical forms and spatial organizations in an abstract manner which refers to aesthetic conventions that were inherited.

[13] Lotfy 1940, 47

libraries with emphasis on the lavish décor and the different styles of furniture.[14] This tradition persists to the present day.

The existing site constraints also challenged the architects' critical approach to the local norms. The apartment houses were designed to specific site conditions in existing neighborhoods and, as long as these sites allowed basic healthy conditions through good ventilation and adequate sunlight, they suited the architects and were not rejected as un-modern configurations of space. Almost all of the projects designed in the urban center accepted the site conditions and were developed respecting these conditions; hence, we are presented with creative solutions such as multiple high-rise courtyards that allowed maximum external exposure and façade surface. This emphasis on healthy conditions became apparent in the drawings related to these projects.

Of course the claim for healthy environments was emphasized much when dealing with villages and popular neighborhoods. The architects benefited from the situation by competing among each other to design higher, more efficient, more appealing structures. Each design had to "be better than the neighboring ones ... and that [the designs] should be a model for years to come."[15] Additionally, due to social and cultural imperatives of the site, mixed-use schemes continued and developed in more complex forms and the designs were presented in ways that highlighted organizational and functional flexibility. This is clear in examples where the programs define alternative functions for the same floors.[16] Ideas of single-use zoning were only adapted when

---

[14] Arnold Wright, *Twentieth Century Impressions of Egypt: its history, people, commerce, industries and resources* (London: Lloyd's Greater Britain Publishing Company, Ltd..1909), 399

[15] Gabr 1941, 64

[16] In a project published by Sayyid Kurayim, he defined alternative programs for the building.

meaningful. These hybrid attitudes and mixed-use projects only started to disappear by the post-revolutionary, Nassir era when a new definition of modern architecture emerged transforming into a more of a particular nationalist style.

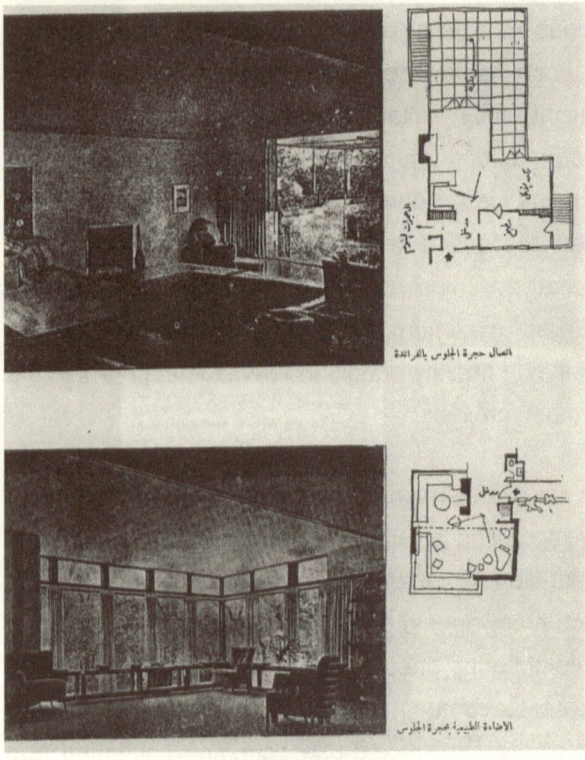

Figure 3. Sketches of the living room published in *al-`imara* showing the design criteria and spatial organization. (Reference: al-`imara 1945)

With regard to spatial organization, Egyptian architects introduced and defined new spaces that were not usual in the Egyptian apartment house. While in earlier models, living activities took place in various rooms in the residence, the modern architects defined specific spaces for such activities. In an article by Salah Zeitoun discussing the importance and the spatial requirements of the living

room as an "important element in the house of our time," he recalled
that it had become a place for "sitting, eating, working, receiving i.e. a
daily living space."[17] In the article he defined its spatial and
organizational characteristics. Up until recently, the term "living room"
(ghorfat jelouss) was rarely used in the architectural drawings of
Egyptian architects. The terms salon (reception) (ghorfat 'istiqbal)
were used instead. It did not have a distinct use and was used
interchangeably with the entrance hall (sallah). By the 1940's this
changed and it gained recognition as a crucial unique space in the
house with specific features in terms of location, ventilation, lighting,
and furnishing.

Changes in the family social structure occurred within these few
decades and the separation between male and female spaces
became less explicit compared to the earlier configuration. Although
the spatial characteristics preserved conservative well defined spaces
as opposed to attempts to "break out of the box," nonetheless, the
manner in which these spaces were inhabited added another level of
complexity to the designs. By the changing attitudes towards family,
spaces that had clear gender roles became more communal and
integrated and the spatial distinctions became more blurred. Hence,
we are faced with traditional spaces that are renamed to
accommodate new functions such as the salamlik which becomes the
office, library or additional reception, elements that seize to exist such
as separate entrances and spaces that become more clearly defined
such as the living rooms.[18]

---

[17] Salah Zeitoun, The Living Room. *Majalit al-'imara*, no.4 & 5(1945): 20

[18] As the journal progressed, new spaces appeared in the plans while others
disappeared. In the earlier (example) libraries which often defined a male space
disappeared and separate reception areas became more integrated.

In addition to the existing larger units, more compact residential designs became more common. Changes from the multi-nuclear family structure to the nuclear family allowed such spatial transformations to occur. Although, these changes began early in the century, by the 1940's the definition of the family revolved around the nuclear family.[19] This is clear in many middle class apartment houses which only accommodated 2-3 bedrooms. The new compact apartment houses allowed more diversification of the urban landscape. More choice was available for different forms of family to coexist. Spaces that defined social class, however, did not change much; hence we find that the service circulation and ancillary spaces, such as the kitchen and laundries, maintain a clear separation from the rest of the unit. The kitchens were located on service courtyards with separate access and the laundry units were located on the roofs maintaining complete separation from the main familial spaces.

Similarly, façades went through major changes in treatment and form and began to promote a new aesthetic in Egyptian urbanism. According to Tawfik Abdel-Gawad:

The modern attitude towards simplifying forms and building codes has greatly affected façade designs by simplifying them also. Facades have become planes free of ornament and cornices at the same time the architect relies now on beautiful proportions and new

---

[19] Sayid Kuyraim ed. al-Bi'a al-mi`maria wa manazil al-'athria'. Edited by K. al-Nigmy. 2 vols. Vol. no. 1, *Sijil al-Hilal al-Mussawir*. Al-qahira: Dar al-Hilal, 1992, mentions that the age of the multi-nuclear extended family in which three generations live together was gone and this led to more demand of smaller residences and apartment houses (`*imarat*). This also led to the disappearance of te separate kitchen in the traditional manner. He also relates the emergence of windows to more female independence. As I mention in my paper, the windows as a spatial type appear much early than the 1930s. The complexity of this must be acknowledged.

materials and applied them in different areas of the building. He also relied on protrusions, balconies, and verandas..."[20]

A general acceptance of simplicity, building codes and new materials affected the facades formal characteristics. The new materials, especially reinforced concrete instead of load bearing masonry, allowed a new approach to form through features such as wide openings, plain surfaces and large cantilevered verandas. However, Abdel-Gawad maintained that these formal innovations should not negatively affect the privacy of the neighbors by being too close or intrusive. Interestingly in various cases the conventional tripartite division of the façade mentioned earlier in the paper was maintained, in an abstract and implicit manner by protrusions and recesses. As a result of the formal treatments and the new construction methods, the horizontality of the facades was accentuated and emphasized in an unprecedented manner. These formal characteristics began to dominate the Cairo urbanism and in the 1950's, by the publication of the first Arabic pattern book, Donia al-Mabani (1952), these forms were popularized and mediated to another degree beyond what had been done in the 15 years of the late 30's and 40's, and a new paradigm was about to dictate Egyptian architecture and urbanism[21]

The interests of the architects and their critical attitudes towards the surrounding influences can be illustrated through an analysis of examples of building programs published. These programs not only provide insights into the design specifics; they also exemplify the priorities and what social, aesthetic and spatial aspects were necessary to communicate with the general public. Furthermore, they illustrate the aesthetics and concepts that the Egyptian modernists

---

[20] Abdel-Gawad 1952, 36

[21] Ahmed Salama, Donia al-Mabani (1952)

cared to emphasize. Through analyzing the components of the program and the overall format of the text, more light will be shed on what the Egyptian architects regarded as crucial and what was trivial in modern architecture.

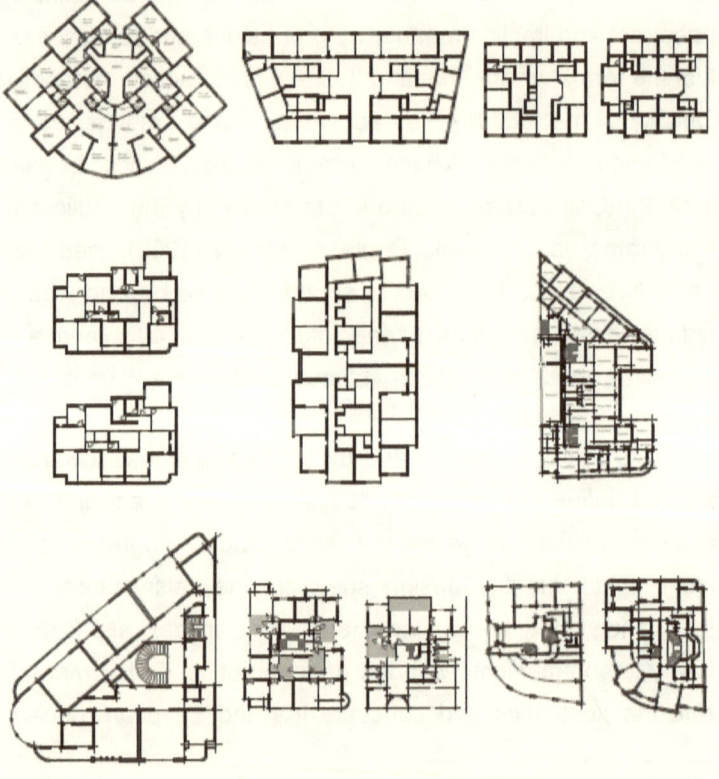

Analyzing the Spatial Layout of Subsidized Apartments in the US

Análise das arranjos espaciais de apartmanentos subsidiados nos EUA

Gavet Douangvichit

Durante todo o ano de 2008 Gavet Douangvichit coletou e analisou dezenas de apartamentos subsidiados, os chamados "public housing" nos EUA. O resultado apresentado aqui neste artigo reitera algumas das hipóteses levantadas durante as reuniões do Global Apartments Research Group de que os EUA representam a principal excessão quandos e trata de apartamentos. Em primeiro lugar porque apartamentos em áreas centrais dos EUA raramente são habitados por famílias com filhos (exceto em New York ou Portland) sendo portanto dirigidos para solteiros, jovens casais e idosos, o que em sí já os diferencia do resto do mundo. Em segundo lugar a área média das residências nos Estados Unidos esteve crescendo aceleradamente nas últimas décadas (vai provalmente arrefecer entre 2008-2010) alcançando a cifra de 190 m2 de média enquanto nos países Europeus a média não passa de 120m2 e nos países em desenvolvimento fica sempre abaixo de 100m2. Tudo isso colabora para que os apartamentos norte-americanos sejam dificilmente comparáveis aos do resto do mudo, exceto que quando se trata de apartamentos subsidiados pelo poder público cuja população são as famílias de baixa renda e a comparação, como mostra esse artigo, fica mais viável.

The data presented in this paper encompasses the spatial analysis of 25 subsidized housing floor plans and 20 market floor plans in a variety of American cities. The subsidized plans in the study are comprised of units designed for single families and do not consider the elderly or the disabled. The analysis includes calculations of each apartment's total square footage, including area calculations of social space (dining, living and family room), service space (kitchen, bath and laundry), private space (bedrooms), circulation space, and veranda/porch/balcony space. In addition to area calculations, each apartment's spatial depth is computed. The spatial depth is determined by the number of rooms through which one must traverse in order to reach a particular space. For example, if one must travel through 2 spaces in order to arrive at a particular room, that room has a spatial depth of 3 (an additional point is included for the room itself). The final spatial depth is the average of all the spatial depth values in the floor plan.[1] Using the collected data from both subsidized and market rate apartment plans, a comparison can be made to define similarities and differences between the two apartment types and speculate on the defining characteristics of subsidized housing plans relative to the rest of the market.

Before the 1930s, there existed only a few examples of housing projects to assist low-income dwellers in the United States. It was in 1917 that the federal government first engaged in housing assistance. The first efforts included funding the construction of housing facilities and providing loans to limited-dividend housing corporations to construct housing units for defense workers (Ledbetter 491).

---

[1] See Methodology(pags 29-41) for more information on the Global Apartments process.

In the 1930s, the Great Depression was responsible for many government initiatives to stimulate the economy and improve public welfare. After the stock market crashed in 1929, the Federal Housing Administration was able to assist moderate- to high-income families secure lower interest rates on their home mortgages, but improvements for low-income families required more effort (Schonauer 388). In 1940, "19 percent of the existing housing stock needed major repairs; 46 percent of all dwelling units had no private bath; 22 percent had no gas or electricity; 30 percent lacked a refrigerator; and 12 percent had no central heating or stoves" (Schonauer 388). To fund the building of more and better homes for the lower class, Congress enabled the Reconstruction Finance Corporation (RFC) to administer loans to limited-dividend housing corporations. The loans resulted in 1 built work, although 600 projects were initiated. Despite the lack of progress, the RFC paved the way for future private and local initiatives in the following years of early public housing (Pommer 236). On March 13, 1935, Senator Robert F. Wagner of New York urged Congress to pass a bill to form a low-rent public housing administration. Wagner defended the bill by claiming it would mitigate many problems caused by the Great Depression, including unemployment and slum neighborhoods (Ledbetter 492). After a lengthy debating process, the bill was passed by the House of Representatives on August 18, 1935.

The passing of the Housing Act on September 1, 1937 marked a critical moment in the history of subsidized housing. This act created a new subdivision within the Department of Interior: the United States Housing Authority (USHA). This agency lent and granted funds to local government housing authorities, as well as delineated the minimum construction and maintenance standards for public housing (Rowe 388). After its creation, USHA moved from the Department of Interior to the Federal Works Agency, and later shifted again, to the

National Housing Agency (Ledbetter 492). During this same time, the public housing sector became the Public Housing Administration (PHA). In 1949, the National Housing Agency was replaced by the Housing and Home Finance Agency and the PHA was absorbed into this new agency (Ledbetter 492).

Another important player in the housing program was added in 1965 with the approval of the Housing and Urban Development Act. This act created the Department of Housing and Urban Development (HUD), which develops and executes housing policies (Ledbetter 492). HUD has since been active in a number of housing initiatives ranging from Community Planning and Development, which organizes affordable housing and homelessness programs, to Fair Housing and Equal Opportunity, which enforces Federal laws against discrimination of minority households and persons with disabilities. For the purposes of research, HUD is a valuable resource for current data concerning the characteristics of housing units and its residents.

A Comparative Spatial Analysis

The floor plans for the subsidized and market rate apartments reveal some interesting and unexpected comparisons. The spatial analysis provided the following mean values for area calculations:

	Subsidized	Market Rate
Total Area	844.61	1190.78
Social Area	254.60	417.09
Service Area	193.12	263.03
Private Area	291.90	387.02
Circulation	69.49	100.14
Veranda/Porch	35.51	23.62
Spatial Depth	2.78	2.35

The following graphs represent the area calculations for subsidized and market rate apartments:

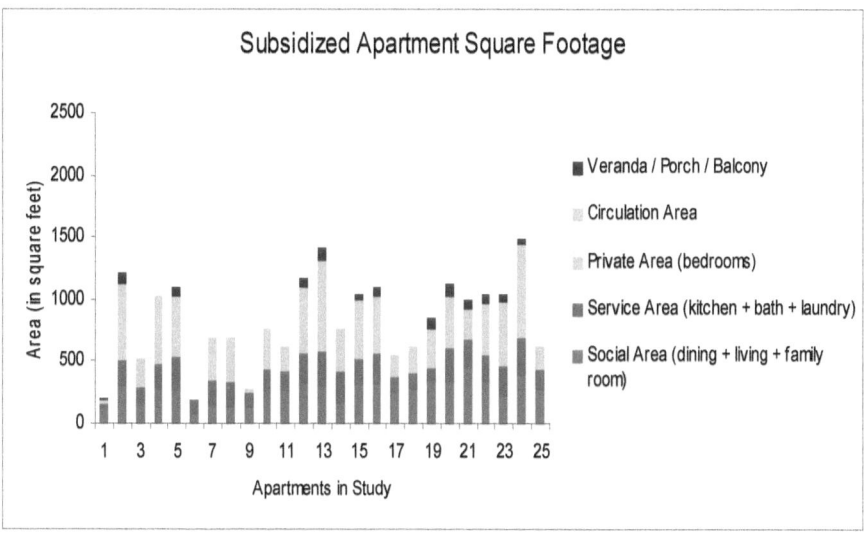

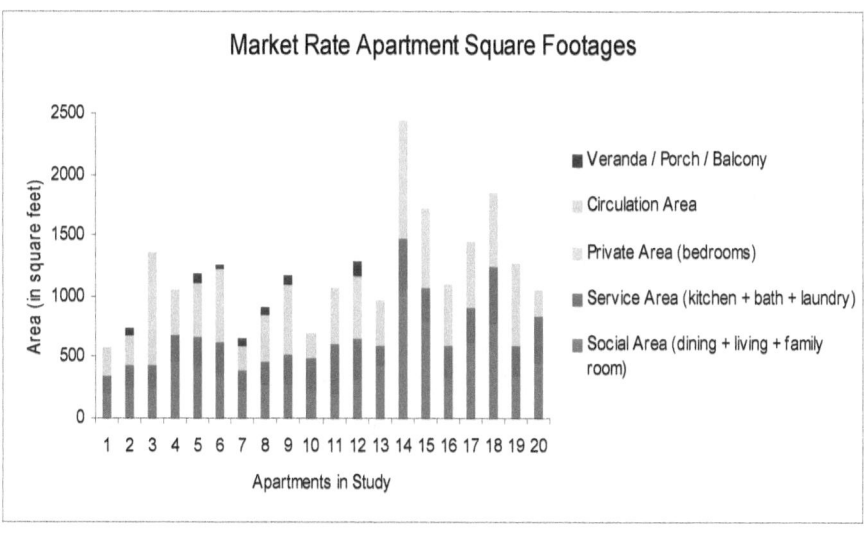

The following graphs represent the spatial depths for subsidized and market rate apartments:

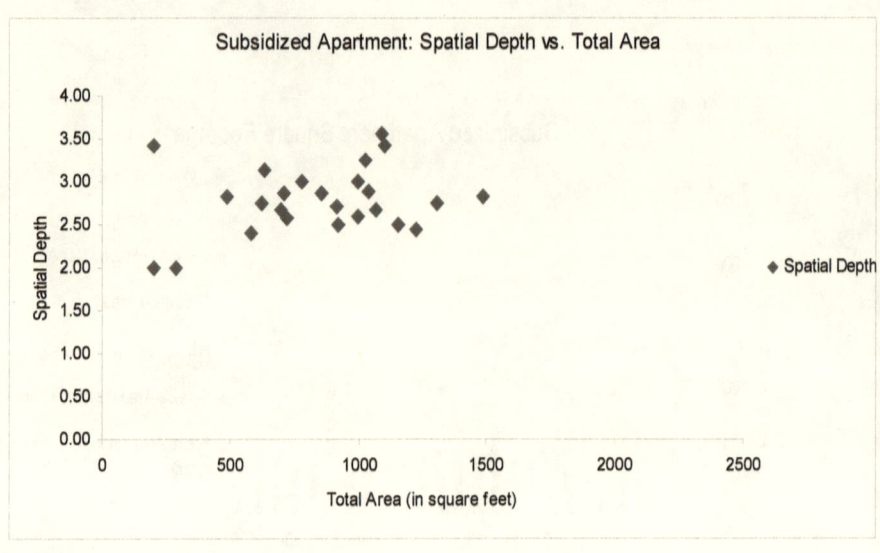

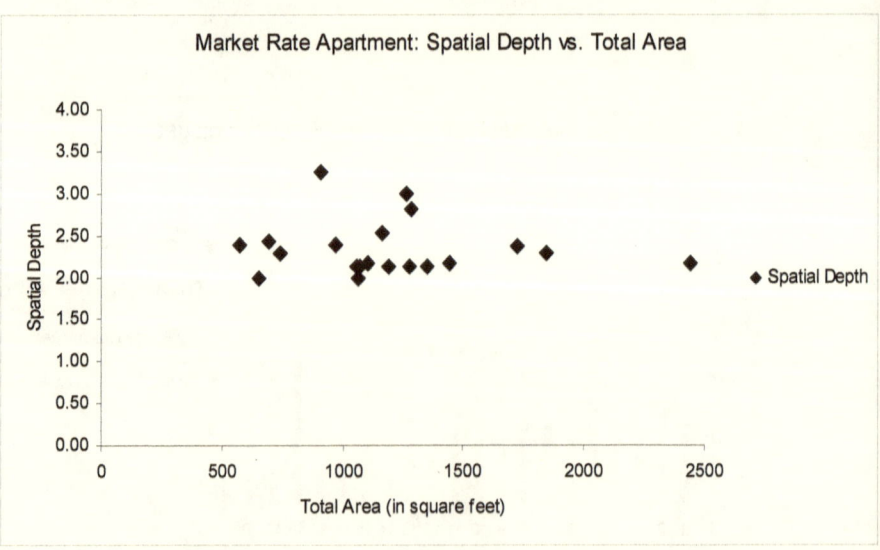

The average values found from the area calculations show that, in general, the spaces in unsubsidized apartments are larger than in subsidized apartments, with the exception of veranda/porch/balcony space. Based on the average values, the total area of a market rate apartment is 40.99% larger than that of a subsidized apartment. Comparing the remaining average area calculations, the market rate social area is 63.82% larger than the subsidized social area, the market rate service area is 36.20% larger than the subsidized service area, the market rate private area is 32.59% larger than the subsidized private area, and the market rate circulation area is 44.11% larger than the subsidized circulation area. The subsidized veranda/porch/balcony space is 50.34% larger than the market rate veranda/porch/balcony space. Although the spaces in subsidized apartments are typically smaller, the proportion of those spaces relative to the total area of the apartment is similar to that of a market rate apartment.

From the percentages, it appears that the greatest difference in spatial partitioning happens between private and social spaces. Relative to the total area, market rate apartments allocate a larger space for social use than seen in subsidized apartments. At 36% of the total area, the market rate social space comprises the largest percentage of the space in the apartment. In contrast, the subsidized apartment dedicates the largest percentage of space to the private area, which is 35% of the total area. The discrepancy between the spatial layouts of the two apartment types may or may not be credited to the actual use of the space. It may be the case that the design of the layout does not reflect the occupant's best use of space. In other words, that a room is larger does not mean that it is used more often. It may be larger simply by design.

The spatial depth comparison between the two apartment types is relatively significant. In this data set, the average spatial depth for subsidized apartments is 2.78, whereas the average spatial depth for market rate apartments is 2.35. The total area of subsidized apartments is smaller than the total area of market rate apartments, yet the subsidized apartments have a greater spatial depth, indicating that a larger total area does not necessitate a greater spatial depth. In fact, if one looks at the subsidized data alone, it shows that as the total area becomes larger, the spatial depth stays generally the same. If one looks at the market rate data alone, one can see that there is a cluster of apartments in the 750 sq.ft. – 1500 sq.ft. range that have higher spatial articulation than the rest of the apartments. There is also a concentration of data points within this range, illustrating that most of the apartments fall within these sizes. It appears from the data that the most common apartment sizes exhibit the highest articulation of space. This result also indicates that for the market rate apartments, more space does not lead to a higher spatial depth.

It is important to understand that greater spatial depth does not equal greater spatial complexity, nor does it mean better design. While the calculation of spatial depth is useful to illustrate the level of accessibility that each space possesses, it does not address other qualities that contribute to spatial complexity, namely spatial arrangement. A space can have a high spatial depth yet still be considered spatially simple. In addition, the definition of spatial complexity is subjective.

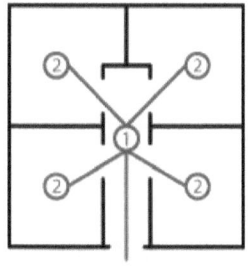   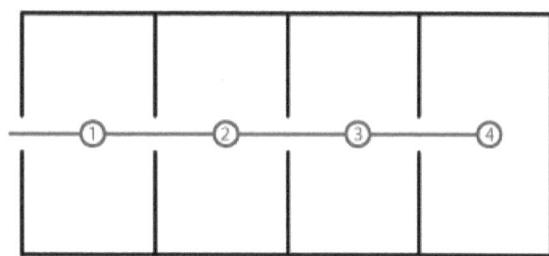

Example A   Example B

Note that although example A has more spaces than example B, it has a lower spatial depth. Example B has one room that reaches a spatial depth of 4, while example A's maximum depth is 2. Does this comparison mean B has a greater spatial complexity than A? Or, is the reverse true, since A has a higher number of spaces?

To further illustrate the concept of spatial depth relative to spatial quality, it may be useful to look at an example from the data set.

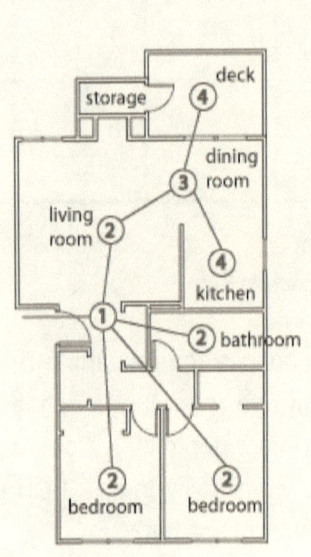

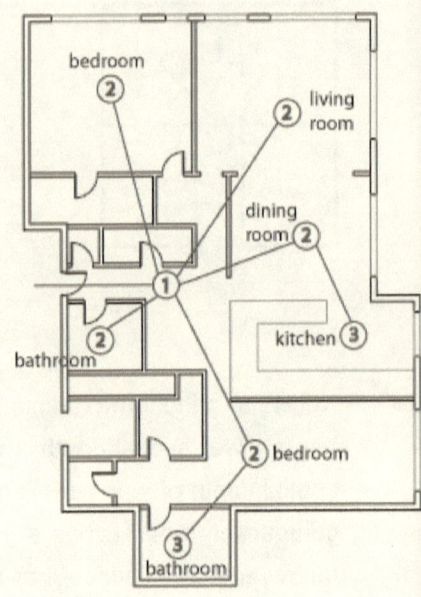

Example C
Subsidized Apartment
Tacoma, Washington
2 Bedroom
Total Area = 920 sq.ft.
Spatial Depth = 2.5

Example D
Market Rate Apartment
Tacoma, Washington
2 Bedroom
Total Area = 1275 sq.ft.
Spatial Depth = 2.125

Here, both plans have 8 spatial divisions, excluding closets (storage space is considered closet space). Although Example C has a smaller total area, it has a greater spatial depth than Example D, again illustrating that increased area does not lead to increased spatial articulation. Note, however, that although example D has a smaller spatial depth, it has a greater number of interior walls, totaling 14. Example C only contains 10 interior walls. This observation is interesting for a few reasons. First, spatial layering in the subsidized apartment is achieved through a small number of interior constructions. In this sense, the layout would be more cost efficient than one with more walls but the same spatial depth. Second, it is not necessarily the case that spatial layering is the most efficient living space, as it is likely more comfortable to navigate through an apartment that contains spaces with easy access to other spaces. Example D may have a smaller spatial depth, but one could say that it is able to achieve spatial divisions without increasing the distance that one must travel to get to a different location. In particular, the living and dining area of the apartment appear easily and equally accessible from the hallway, yet the construction of a wall between the dining room and the hallway offers an additional spatial partition, as well as creates a walking path to the living room. Lastly, the layout of walls in the subsidized apartment seems to follow a tighter grid than seen in the market rate apartment. It appears as if a series of volumes were deposited into the layout and retrofitted to accommodate the greater shape. In the market rate apartment, the partitions emerge as more loosely arranged volumes, shifting around the grid to accommodate other adjacent spaces. As a consequence of design, the looser grid requires more walls than the tighter one.

The strict grid of the subsidized apartment leads to particular spatial arrangements. As a result of the adherence to the grid, the spaces are more compartmentalized than those in the market rate apartment. The compartmentalization suggests a higher level of privacy for the people in the spaces. As seen in the earlier pie charts, it is also true that (relative to total area) the subsidized apartment dedicates more square footage to the bedrooms, a private domain in the home. The focus on privacy is then applied to other parts of the apartment as well. As seen in image C, the kitchen has a spatial depth of 4, indicating a higher level of privacy for that space because it is less accessible than the other spaces. In image D, the kitchen has a comparable spatial depth at 3, but it is seen from the plan that the kitchen is more spatially open. Since there is no wall between the entry area and the kitchen, the kitchen is one of the first spaces that an occupant encounters when s/he enters the space. Thus, although the kitchen has a spatial depth of 3, the way in which it occupies the space offers visual accessibility, which diminishes the privacy that may otherwise be associated with a room that has a high spatial depth. As seen from the pie charts, the market rate apartment designates the most space to social area relative to the total area of the apartment. This allocation indicates an emphasis on social rather than private space.

The social emphasis in market rate apartments may be associated with the demographic living in these apartments. In America, the most desirable home for a family is a house, and most middle- to high-income families live in houses. As a result, apartments are not usually designed for families because it is assumed that families strive to live in houses. The apartment is treated as the temporary abode and is targeted toward college students and young professionals or singles. The lifestyle of a youth is often socially focused, and the design of market rate apartments lends itself to be a space of entertaining. The flexible plan with easy access to adjacent spaces creates a suitable social environment, enabling the occupants to move more freely in the space. It accommodates social activity by allowing the occupants to encounter one anther in a number of ways. Note for instance the position of the dining space in Example D. One can enter this space from the kitchen, living room or directly from the hall. In Example C, one can only reach the dining room after having traveled through the living room. The layout in Example C is more rigid and prescriptive.

The subsidized apartment is designed to be a family dwelling. Low-income families tend to live in apartments because they often lack the financial resources to acquire and maintain a house (e.g. proper credit for loans, ability to pay property taxes, etc.). The subsidized apartment may be less socially focused than the market rate apartment because it makes assumptions about the needs of a family dwelling. In the subsidized layout, there is a focus on partitioned space to allow each member of the family to have more privacy as they occupy the apartment. The higher spatial depth of subsidized apartments indicates that the spaces are more layered, which restricts the freedom of accessibility that is seen in the market rate apartments. However, it is not always the case that members of a family will want more privacy from other members in their home. Also, it is not always true that family members will be less social with each other or entertain guests less often than young professionals living in apartments. In this way, the spatial layout of a subsidized apartment is not necessarily an accurate reflection of family needs and uses.

On the other hand, the subsidized apartment's strict adherence to the grid, which leads to spatial layering, may simply be the desire to minimize cost. If the goal of developers is to build these apartments cheaply, then the use of less material is desirable. Thus, the adherence to the grid may not be an emphasis on privacy as much as a result of budget. That fewer walls lead to less flexibility is the result of sacrificing design for affordability. The cost conscious construction project will always have fewer options than the project with more funds.

Since market rate apartments appear to be designed with cost efficiency in mind, the spaces are simply and orthogonally arranged. It remains to be seen whether this arrangement properly accommodates its occupants. Approximately 43% of families living in subsidized housing contain children, and about 56% of the families are supported by a single parent (Public Housing: Image Versus Fact 1). Approximately 77% of the head of households are female, and 40% of those females have children (Huduser). The average number of people per unit is 2.3 (Huduser). Studio or 1 bedroom apartments comprise 48% of subsidized housing. Approximately 25% of subsidized apartments have 2 bedrooms and 28% have 3 or more bedrooms (Public Housing: Image Versus Fact 3). If 2.3 people per unit is a true reflection of real-life (and not a survey error), and if about half of the subsidized units are 2 bedrooms or more, then overcrowding may not be an issue in subsidized apartments. However, there may be rogue cases where a family of four lives in a 1 bedroom apartment. These instances are difficult to recognize from the data since the data generalizes the population. If families of 2 or three are living in studio or 1 bedroom apartments, then some overcrowding may occur, depending on the size of the total area. Further research in this department is needed to analyze the suitability of subsidized layouts relative to the occupants.

The layout of subsidized housing today originated from designs beginning in the early 1930s between the two World Wars. During this time, "the older traditions of American philanthropic housing, apartment house layout, and Beaux-Arts planning collided with new ideas of housing developed by European modernists in the 1920s and [was] introduced into this country just as the federal housing programs began" (Pommer 235). As previously discussed in this paper, the first government assisted housing programs in the United States were designed to provide housing quarters for defense workers during World War 1. In addition to being influenced by these designs, early public housing was modeled after the Beaux-Arts standard (which originates from the Ecole des Beaux-Arts in Paris), as well as the Garden City plan (a utopian notion originating in Europe where cities are planned and autonomous, with residential, industrial and agricultural components evenly distributed within its landscape) (Pommer 235).

In 1931, Oskar Stonorov initiated a housing plan for the Full Fashioned Hosiery Workers Union, a project meant to aid the many union workers who were suffering from the Great Depression. To get a loan for the project, Stonorov and Alfred Kastner, both German architects, presented a proposal for the Carl Mackley Houses of Philadelphia to the RFC in August 1932. In Stonorov's mind, the project was meant to "teach the workers the virtues of communal effort in raising their standard of living" (Pommer 239). The layout of the complex assumed the ideals of the Garden City model. Stonorov envisioned "no less than three tennis courts, a swimming pool, a garage for the workers' new autos, stores, and a filling station, not to mention the assembly hall or club house, the library and the play rooms on the roofs" (Pommer 239). The inclusion of middle class luxuries in the project was characteristic of the utopian ideals found in European designs. The European influences seen here were also present in earlier American projects concerned with housing the lower class.

Boston was home to some of the earliest efforts to house low-income families. Although these projects were not subsidized by the government, it is worth noting their origin. "The Boston movement and the buildings it produced are related to their parallels in England and, as far as can be ascertained, in New York, which appears to be the only other American city involved in the very earliest phase of the model housing movement" (Zaitzevsky 157). Boston became in need of housing development after the influx of immigrants to America after the Irish potato famine of 1840-1855 (Zaitevsky 157). Boston had no multi-family housing complexes and the city began looking at English models to extract design ideas. The city committee collected plans from the Birkenhead Dock Company for its four-story, 324 family buildings, as well as from other English organizations (Zaitevsky 159). In September of 1853, Charles Eliot Norton and William S. Bullard began work for a housing model on Osborn Place at Pleasant Street. They hired Benjamin F. Dwight and Charles F. Kirby to design the project. The interior of the buildings were comprised of four different layouts, all of which were based on English prototypes (Zaitevsky 161). The units contained a living room with a stove, two or three bedrooms, a sink room and a water closet. Some layouts were more distinctly English than others. Plan no.1 of the Osborn Place buildings revealed a symmetrical plan with a circular cast iron staircase in the middle, distinct of English design (Zaitevsky 161). The plan also conveyed a tight adherence to the grid, with a square layout partitioned into nine equal compartments. The title of this layout was named by the draftsman John Claudius Loudon as the "college for working men" (Zaitevsky 161).

Sunnyside Gardens by the City Housing Corporation in New York also derived European influence. This 1928 project was designed to provide a better living environment than the crowded tenement houses of the same time (Rowe 114). Similar to the Osborn Place buildings, this complex was not a public housing project but still an endeavor to assist the low-income citizen. Its goals encompassed "the building of low-priced houses as first-class homes for lower-income dwellers and development of cooperative methods of home ownership" (Rowe 115). Abiding to a Garden City layout, the project also focused on creating outdoor "play space" and a centrally located communal garden (Rowe 115). To open up the middle of the complex, the buildings were arranged at the perimeter of the site. The interior plans for each apartment unit showed orthogonally arranged spaces following a neat grid.

In conclusion, the layout for public housing is derivative of movements in Europe, such as the Beaux-Arts and Garden City models. The early plans of housing for the poor in Boston and New York show strong ties to the design motives of European movements of the same time. The layouts of some public and other government subsidized apartments demonstrate an adherence to the grid, as was observed in early public housing plans based on European designs. The spatial analysis of the subsidized and market rate apartments exposed some but not many differences in spatial proportionality. The pie charts depicting the area partitions relative to total area were almost identical for the two apartment types, despite the difference in total area. Finding reason for the slight discrepancy in area partitions needs further research, as well as the answer to the question regarding whether the space is properly designed for the occupant.

References:

Ledbetter, William H., Jr. "Public Housing: A Social Experiment Seeks Acceptance." Law and Contemporary Problems. Vol. 32, No. 3, Housing, Part 2: The Federal Role. Duke University School of Law, 1967. 450-527.

Huduser. November 21, 2008. HUD. February 25, 2009 <http://www.huduser.org/publications/pubasst.html>.

Pommer, Richard. The Architecture of Urban Housing in the United States in the Early 1930s. The Journal of the Society of Architectural Historians. Vol. 37, No.4. Society of Architectural Historians, December 1978. 235-264.

"Public Housing: Image Versus Facts." Huduser. February 23, 2009 <http://www.huduser.org/periodicals/ushmc/spring95/spring95.html>.

Rowe, Peter G. Modernity and Housing. Cambridge: The MIT Press, 1993.

Schonauer. Twentieth Century Housing: 1900-1950.

Zaitzevsky, Cynthia. " Housing Boston's Poor: The First Philanthropic Experiments." The Journal of the Society of Architectural Historians. Vol. 42, No. 2. Society of Architectural Historians, May 1983. 157-167.

CONTRIBUTORS:

Fernando Luiz Lara was Assistant Professor of Architecture at the University of Michigan (2004-2009) when he created and directed the Global Apartments Research Group. He now teaches at the University of Texas at Austin

Luiz Amorim and **Claudia Loureiro** are our main reference on research on contemporary Brazilian housing and both teach at the Federal University of Pernambuco, in Recife, Brazil

Adriana Gondran Carvalho da Silva, a native of Florianopolis studied architecture at the Federal University of Santa Catarina and is now working on her PhD at the University of Weimar, Germany, with a DAAD fellowship.

Carolina Chaves is an architect who studied at the Federal University of Paraíba and now is a graduate student at the University of São Paulo in São Carlos, Brazil

Youngchul Kim got his architecture degree from Seoul National University and is finishing his PhD at the University of Michigan.

Suma Pahndi was born in Michigan into a Kanadah family, studied Japanese literature and is now pursing her PhD in Architecture while also getting her design skills sharpened by an MArch degree.

Romil Sheth is a native of Bombay, India, graduated from Michigan's Master in Urban Design and now works with Rahul Mehrotra in Boston.

Vera Baranova is an architect with Rafael Vinoly Architects PC. Born in Moscow Russia, she graduated from Michigan in 2008. She will be starting her graduate studies in architecture at Harvard GSD in Fall 2009.

Omar Baghdady was born in Cairo, graduated as an architect from Cairo University, lives in Denver and is about to finish his PhD on Egyptian modernism at the University of Michigan

Gavet Douangvichit was born in Laos, lived most of her life in New England's public housing, graduated from Skidmore College and is now pursuing her Masters at Michigan